THE ONE COOKBOO[K]

RUSH HOUR SUPERCHEF!

WITH
STEP·BY·STEP
MENUS

Second printing 1987

Library of Congress Catalog No. 83-070952

ISBN 0-9611588-0

Dèanne II, Inc.
#3 Quail Run
Box 82 A, Rt. 4
Carthage, Missouri 64836

Copyright © 1983
Dianne Stafford Mayes and
Dorothy Davenport Stafford

RUSH HOUR SUPERCHEF

Design and illustration by
Jim Jump…Nic Frising and
Main Street Design
San Francisco, California

Printed by

WIMMER BROTHERS

Memphis   Dallas

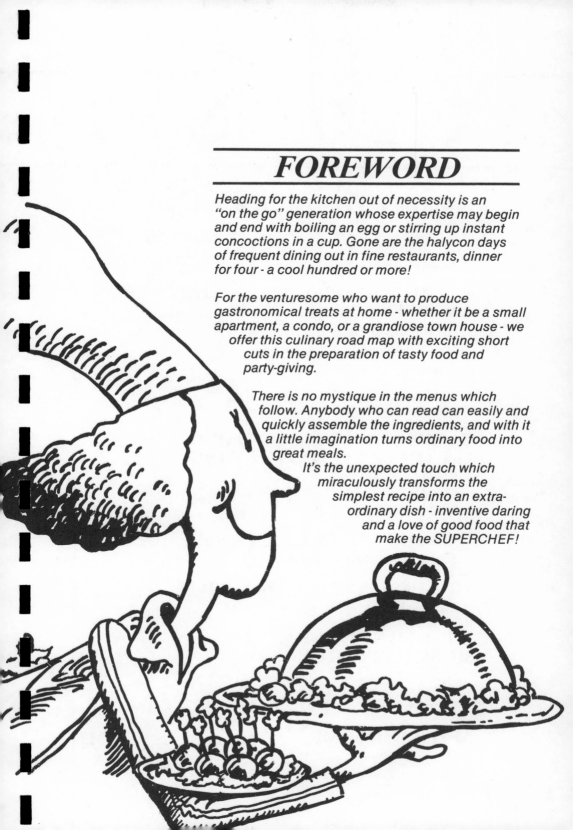

FOREWORD

Heading for the kitchen out of necessity is an "on the go" generation whose expertise may begin and end with boiling an egg or stirring up instant concoctions in a cup. Gone are the halycon days of frequent dining out in fine restaurants, dinner for four - a cool hundred or more!

For the venturesome who want to produce gastronomical treats at home - whether it be a small apartment, a condo, or a grandiose town house - we offer this culinary road map with exciting short cuts in the preparation of tasty food and party-giving.

There is no mystique in the menus which follow. Anybody who can read can easily and quickly assemble the ingredients, and with it a little imagination turns ordinary food into great meals.

It's the unexpected touch which miraculously transforms the simplest recipe into an extra-ordinary dish - inventive daring and a love of good food that make the SUPERCHEF!

C O N T

E N T S

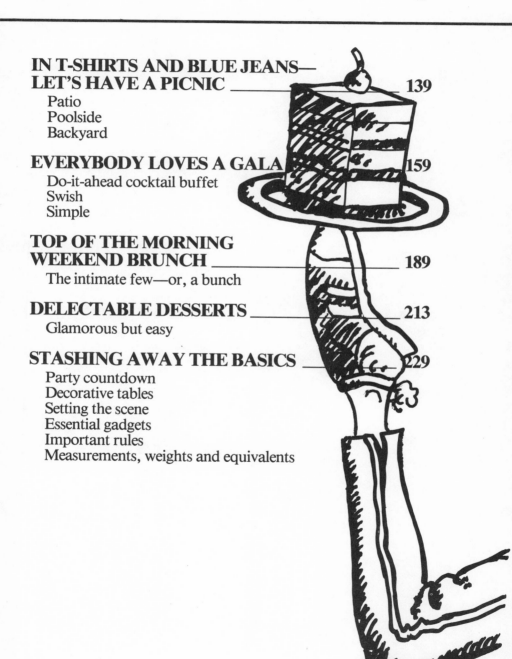

DROP OF A HAT—
DO STOP BY FOR A DRINK

Jiffy Dips · · · · · · · · Jazzed Up Spreads

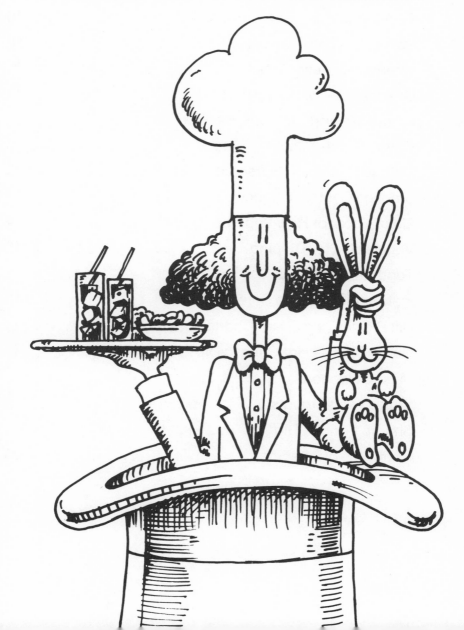

DROP OF A HAT—
DO STOP BY FOR A DRINK

Zesty Italian Tuna Spread

Preparation time: 6 minutes   Makes 2 cups

1 7 oz. can white tuna
½ cup ripe olives
 (buy 3 oz. can)

1 package Good Seasons
 Italian Salad Dressing Mix
1 cup sour cream

1. Drain off oil or water from tuna and rinse meat in cold water.
2. Cut olives in fourths.
3. Combine tuna, olives, salad dressing mix, and sour cream.
4. Stir until well mixed.
5. Place in serving dish, sprinkle with paprika, and serve with crackers (preferably a plain cracker).

Note: If no ripe olives on hand, omit.

Taste of the Sea Clam Dip

Preparation time: 6 minutes   Makes 1 heaping cup

1 7½ oz. can
 minced clams, drained
1 cup sour cream
1 t. dried parsley
⅛ t. onion salt

½ t. Worcestershire sauce
1 t. bottled lemon juice
¼ t. salt
¼ t. Tabasco

1. Mix until well blended: drained clams, sour cream, parsley, onion salt, Worcestershire, lemon juice, salt, and Tabasco.
2. Place in serving bowl, sprinkle lightly with paprika, and garnish with parsley.
3. Refrigerate until ready to use.
4. Serve with potato chips.

Easy Shrimp Spread

Preparation time: 6 minutes   Makes 1 cup

**1 5 oz. can shrimp,
drained (or equivalent
amount of fresh or frozen)**
**1 3 oz. package cream
cheese, softened**
**2 T. mayonnaise
(no substitutes)**
3 t. bottled lemon juice

⅛ t. Worcestershire sauce
¼ t. Tabasco
⅛ t. salt
1 green onion, top only
**¼ cup chopped celery
(optional)**

1. Mince finely top of 1 green onion.
2. Combine cream cheese, mayonnaise, lemon juice, Worcestershire sauce, Tabasco, salt, minced onion top, and celery. Mix well.
3. Fold in drained shrimp and mix gently.
4. Place in serving dish, sprinkle with paprika, garnish with parsley, and refrigerate until ready to serve.
5. Serve with crackers.

Note: If using fresh or frozen shrimp, chop finely.

Savory Deviled Ham

Preparation time: 6 minutes   Makes 1 cup

1 2½ oz. can deviled ham
¼ cup sour cream
½ t. bottled lemon juice
½ t. Dijon mustard

⅛ t. Worcestershire sauce
**¼ cup chopped green
pepper (optional)**

1. Combine ham, sour cream, lemon juice, mustard, Worcestershire sauce, and chopped green pepper.
2. Stir until well mixed.
3. Place in serving dish, garnish with additional green pepper slivers, and refrigerate until ready to serve.
4. Serve with crackers.

Cheddar Cheese Snap I

Preparation time: 6 minutes   Makes 1 cup

**1 4 oz. package shredded
sharp Cheddar cheese
1½ T. mayonnaise
(no substitutes)**

**3 green onions minced
(more tops than bottoms)
½ t. Dijon mustard
¼ t. Tabasco**

1. Mince onions finely.
2. Combine cheese, mayonnaise, onions, mustard, and Tabasco, mixing well.
3. Form into a mound.
4. Sprinkle with paprika, garnish with parsley, and serve with crackers.

Cheddar Cheese Snap II

Preparation time: 6 minutes   Makes 1 cup

**1 4 oz. package shredded
sharp Cheddar cheese
⅓ cup sour cream
⅛ t. Tabasco**

**¼ t. salt
⅛ t. coarsely ground
black pepper
¼ t. Accent**

1. Combine all ingredients and stir until well mixed.
2. Form into a mound.
3. Cover tightly and refrigerate until ready to use.
4. Sprinkle with paprika, garnish with parsley sprigs, and serve with crackers.

Mouth-Melting Bleu Cheese Spread

Preparation time: 6 minutes   Makes 1¼ cups

**2 oz. crumbled bleu cheese
(buy a 4 oz. carton
and use half)
1 3 oz. package cream
cheese, softened**

**1 cup sour cream
2 t. dry white wine
½ cup chopped walnuts
(optional)**

1. Combine all ingredients and mix until well blended.
2. Place in small bowl and surround with crackers.
3. Sprinkle with paprika and garnish with parsley.

Crisp Stuffed Celery

Preparation time: 10 minutes   Makes 12 individual appetizers

4 celery stalks

**1 small jar pimento cheese
spread**

1. Wash, clean, and towel dry celery.
2. Cut each stalk into 3 equal pieces.
3. Stuff celery ribs with cheese spread or Mouth Melting
   Bleu Cheese Spread.
4. Sprinkle with paprika and garnish with parsley or
   celery leaves.

Chipped Beef and Horseradish

Preparation time: 7 minutes   Makes 1¼ cups

**1 3 oz. package cream
cheese, softened
⅔ cup sour cream
1 2½ oz. package dried
chipped beef**

**⅛ t. dried minced onion
1 t. Dijon mustard
1 t. horseradish (hot)**

1. Tear chipped beef in small pieces and place in blender or food processor.
2. Add cream cheese, sour cream, onion, mustard, and horseradish.
3. Turn on high and mix well. (Scrape down sides 2 or 3 times and reblend if necessary.)
4. Place in serving dish, sprinkle with paprika, and garnish with ripe olives.
5. Chill until ready to serve.
6. Serve with Triscuits.

Smoked Oyster Canapes

Preparation time: 6 minutes   Serves 4

1 3 oz. package cream cheese, softened
½ T. mayonnaise (no substitutes)
⅛ t. salt

¼ t. bottled lemon juice
1 3¾ oz. can smoked oysters
Triscuits

1. Drain oysters
2. Combine cream cheese, mayonnaise, salt, and lemon juice.
3. Mix until smooth.
4. Spread cream cheese mixture over Triscuits, top with an oyster, and garnish with parsley sprig.

Option: Mound cream cheese on tray surrounded by oysters speared on toothpicks and Triscuits. Let guests serve themselves.

Quick Dips for Raw Vegetables and Chips
Dip I

Preparation time: 5 minutes   Makes 1½ cups

1 8 oz. package cream cheese, softened

½ cup sour cream

1 package Good Seasons Bleu Cheese Salad Dressing Mix

1. Combine all ingredients and mix well with fork until thoroughly blended.
2. Place in serving dish and refrigerate until ready to use.

Dip II

Preparation time: 5 minutes   Makes 1½ cups

1 8 oz. package cream cheese, softened

½ cup sour cream

1 package Good Seasons Green Goddess Salad Dressing Mix

1. Combine all ingredients and mix well with a fork until thoroughly blended.
2. Pour into attractive serving bowl and refrigerate until ready to use.

Note: This dip is also good with shrimp.

Dip III

Preparation time: 5 minutes   Makes 2 cups

1 8 oz. package cream cheese, softened

1 cup mayonnaise (no substitutes)

1 1-oz. package Hidden Valley Ranch Salad Dressing Mix

1. Combine all ingredients and mix well with fork until thoroughly blended.
2. Place in serving dish and refrigerate until ready to use.
3. At serving time sprinkle lightly with paprika and surround with fresh vegetables or potato chips.

Vegetables for Dipping

Broccoli and cauliflower separated into flowerettes

Green pepper cut into strips

Button mushrooms

Carrots cut into sticks

Celery stalks cut into sticks

Zucchini thinly sliced

Cherry tomatoes

Toothpick Quickies

Preparation time: 7 minutes for 16 individual appetizers
Makes as many as you wish

1 4-6 oz. block Swiss cheese

1 3 oz. jar pickled cocktail onions

bite sized ham cubes (optional)

toothpicks

1. Cut cheese and ham into ½" to ¾" cubes.
2. Spear a pickled onion on a toothpick, follow with cube of ham, cube of cheese, and another pickled onion.
3. Place on a tray and garnish with parsley.

Instant Pickapeppa Spread

Preparation time: 5 minutes   Serves as many as you wish

**1 5 oz. bottle Pickapeppa
Sauce**
**1 3 oz. package cream
cheese, softened**

crackers

1. Mound softened cream cheese in center of tray or plate.
2. Sprinkle with paprika and garnish with parsley.
3. Pour Pickapeppa Sauce into small bowl and place with
   spoon on same tray with cream cheese.
4. Surround with crackers and let guests spread cream
   cheese on crackers and top with Pickapeppa Sauce.

Dill Pickles and Sharp Cheddar

Preparation time: 7 minutes   Serves as many as you wish

**1 6-8 oz. block sharp
Cheddar cheese**
**1 jar chilled and crisp
dill pickles**

crackers (optional)

1. Slice as many cheese slices as number to be served.
2. Cut whole dill pickles into 4 slices lengthwise and then
   in half again.
3. Lay one pickle on top of each cheese slice. (Crackers
   are not necessary if cheese slices are generous.)
4. Place on tray or dish, garnish with parsley, and serve.

SUCCULENT...EASY...AND...HOT

Green Chili-Hot Cheese Dip

Preparation time: 10 minutes   Makes 1½ cups

1 8 oz. carton Green Chili dip
1 4 oz. package Velveeta cheese

1 4 oz. chopped mild green chili peppers, drained
¼ t. Tabasco

1. Tear cheese into small pieces and place in saucepan.
2. Add Green Chili dip and heat until cheese is melted.
3. Add Tabasco and chopped chili peppers.
4. Pour into bowl and serve with Doritos, Fritos, or melba toast.

Minute Nachos

Preparation time: ½ minute per nacho
Cooking time: 1-1½ minutes   Serves: As many as you like

1 box Nachips
1 6 oz. package "squeeze a snak" garlic flavor cheese

Tabasco
1 6 oz. can frozen avocado dip, thawed (Calavo recommended)

1. Preheat broiler.
2. Cover each Nachip with a generous squeeze of garlic flavored cheese.
3. Sprinkle with 1-2 drops Tabasco.
4. Broil 5" from heat 1-1½ minutes, or until cheese melts.
5. Top each Nachip with 1 t. avocado dip and serve immediately.

Stuffed Mushrooms

Preparation time: 10 minutes
Cooking time: 10-15 minutes
Makes 16 individual stuffed mushrooms

16 medium sized fresh mushrooms
1 3 oz. package cream cheese, softened
1 T. cream (or milk)
1 t. minced dried chives (or 2 t. finely minced green onions)

1 t. bottled lemon juice
⅛ t. salt
scant ⅛ t. white pepper
1½ T. butter

1. Preheat oven to 350 degrees.
2. Put butter in shallow baking dish and place in oven to melt.
3. Wash and dry mushrooms and remove center stem.
4. Combine cream cheese, milk, chives, lemon juice, salt, and pepper.
5. Mix with a fork until all ingredients are thoroughly combined and mixture is smooth.
6. Mound cream cheese mixture in center of each mushroom and sprinkle lightly with paprika for color.
7. Place mushrooms in melted butter, return to oven and bake 10-15 minutes — just until heated through.
8. Place on serving tray, garnish with parsley, and spear each mushroom with a colored toothpick. Serve.

Shrimp Fondue Dip

Preparation time: 10 minutes   Makes 2 cups

**1 can condensed cream
  of shrimp soup**
1 6 oz. roll garlic cheese

1 t. bottled lemon juice
¼ t. Tabasco

1. Place soup and cheese in saucepan over medium high heat to melt.
2. Stir in lemon juice and Tabasco when melted.
3. Place in chafing dish or oven proof container and serve with melba toast.

Hurry Ups off the Shelf

Popcorn

Ripe olives or green pimento-stuffed olives

Mixed nuts

Sesame sticks

Dry roasted peanuts

Marinated mushrooms speared on toothpicks

Assortment of dried fruits

Crunchy potato or other kind of chips

Peanuts and raisins mixed

MOUTH-WATERING SOUPS, CHOWDERS, AND BREWS

Off the Shelf . . . Out of a can!

SOUPS...CHOWDERS...AND BREWS

Mouth-watering hot and cold concoctions off the shelf, out of a can, and ladled from pot to guests around the kitchen table . . . hot soups fiery hot, cold icy cold.

No soup bowls? Use giant coffee mugs for hot soups and chowders; long stemmed and chilled wine glasses for cold.

Add crusty chunks of bread or crackers and you have a satisfying meal-in-a-bowl. Toss in a simple salad or fruit and cheese, and "Voila," you have a repast!

IMPORTANT! When using canned soups, use wire whisk to blend soup ingredients.

TAKE YOUR CHOICE CLAM CHOWDERS!

Clam Chowder New England Style

Preparation time: 10 minutes   Serves 4 heartily

2 6½ oz. cans minced clams

2 15 oz. cans Snow's Clam Chowder

1 14½ oz. can Swanson's Chicken Broth

1 t. minced dried chives

⅔ cup cream (or Half and Half)

⅛ t. Tabasco

1 t. dried parsley flakes

¼ t. coarsely ground black pepper

1½ T. sherry

1. Drain clams and pour liquid into soup pot.
2. Combine all ingredients except clams and sherry and bring to a boil.
3. Reduce heat. Simmer 5 minutes stirring constantly.
4. Add clams and sherry, stirring well.
5. Pour into hot soup bowls.

Note: If making ahead of time or freezing, omit pepper and Tabasco and add when serving.

Manhattan Clam Chowder

Preparation time: 12 minutes   Serves 6

2 6½ oz. cans minced clams

2 10¾ oz. cans Chicken Gumbo soup

1 10¾ oz. can Cream of Potato soup

1 16 oz. can tomatoes, undrained

1 cup water

2 t. minced dried onions

1½ t. coarsely ground black pepper

1. Drain clam juice into soup pot.
2. Add soups, tomatoes with liquid, water, onions, and pepper to clam juice.
3. Stir well and bring to a boil.
4. Reduce heat and simmer 8 minutes, stirring occasionally.
5. Add clams and serve.

Ham and Virginia Pea Soup

Preparation time: 10 minutes
Serves 2 heartily, 3 well, 4 in small bowls

2 envelopes Lipton's Virginia Pea instant soup

1 can Cream of Celery soup

1½ cups water

1 2¼ oz. can deviled ham

½ T. sherry (optional)

1. Combine all ingredients except sherry and bring to a boil.
2. Reduce heat and simmer 3 minutes, stirring constantly.
3. Stir in sherry and serve.

Sicilian Consomé

Preparation time: 10 minutes   Serves 4

2 14 oz. cans Swanson's Beef Bouillon
1 soup can water
2 eggs well beaten
salt and pepper to taste

4 T. grated Parmesan or Cheddar cheese
1 T. bottled lemon juice
4 thin slices lemon (optional)

1. Combine bouillon and water.
2. Heat to boiling.
3. Beat eggs in separate bowl until smooth.
4. Stir grated cheese into bouillon.
5. Add lemon juice.
6. Slowly pour boiling stock over beaten eggs and whisk until absorbed.
7. Float a thin slice of lemon sprinkled with minced parsley on top of each serving. (Optional)

Tomato Fromage

Preparation time: 10 minutes
Serves 2 heartily, 3 well, 4 in small bowls

5 slices Velveeta cheese
1 10¾ oz. can Tomato soup
1 soup can water

½ t. basil
1 t. Dijon mustard
½ t. Jane's Seasoning salt

1. Tear cheese in pieces for quick melting and place in pan along with water and soup.
2. Heat over medium high heat stirring constantly with wire whisk until cheese has melted.
3. Add basil, mustard, and seasoning salt.
4. Stir well and serve piping hot.

Dilled Potato Soup

Preparation time: 10 minutes
Serves 2 heartily, 3 well, 4 in small bowls

**1 10¾ oz. can Cream of
Potato soup**
1 soup can milk
dash white pepper

⅛ t. salt
1 t. dried dill
⅔ cup sour cream

1. Mix soup, milk, pepper, salt, and dill in soup pan.
2. Heat until hot, stirring constantly with wire whisk.
3. Stir in sour cream.
4. Pour into soup bowls and sprinkle with paprika for color.

Super-Quick French Onion Soup

Preparation time: 15-18 minutes   Serves 2 heartily, 3 well

1 14½ oz. can Swanson's pure beef broth

2 cups water

1 package Lipton or Knorr Onion Soup Mix and Dip Mix

3 T. instant minced onions

½ T. dry Vermouth

1 Pepperidge Farm french roll or equivalent

Monterey Jack cheese

Parmesan cheese

1. Preheat oven to 350 degrees.
2. Combine beef broth, water, onion soup mix, and minced onion in pan and bring to boil.
3. Reduce heat to simmer.
4. Cut french roll into cubes and pop in oven for 12 minutes.
5. Let soup simmer 10 minutes.
6. Add Vermouth and pour into warm oven proof bowls.
7. Divide cubed french bread evenly among bowls and top with thin slices of Monterey Jack cheese — 3 to 4 slices per bowl.
8. Sprinkle Parmesan cheese lightly over top.
9. Pop under broiler until cheese begins to melt.

Note: If not serving immediately, place soup in warm 200 degree oven and garnish with bread and cheese at last minute.
For a filling meal, serve with salad and hunks of buttered crusty bread.

Cheese Broccoli Soup

Preparation time: 12 minutes   Serves 4

1 10 oz. package chopped frozen Green Giant or Bird's Eye broccoli, thawed and drained (cheaper brands can sometimes be tough)

1 10¾ oz. can condensed Cheddar Cheese soup

1 soup can milk

½ t. salt

⅛ t. pepper

1 t. bottled lemon juice

4 drops Tabasco

6 slices Velveeta cheese

1. Tear cheese in pieces and place in pan with soup and milk.
2. Heat on medium low until cheese is melted and well blended into soup.
3. Add broccoli, salt, pepper, lemon juice and Tabasco.
4. Cook over medium high, stirring constantly, until broccoli is tender.

Cream of Crunchy Peanut Soup

Preparation time: 8 minutes   Serves 4

4 T. butter

½ T. flour

2 cups Swanson's Chicken Broth

1 cup Half and Half

½ t. instant minced onion

¼ t. celery salt

¾ cup crunchy peanut butter

sour cream (for garnish)

1. Melt butter over medium heat.
2. Add flour and cook until well blended.
3. Add chicken broth, onion, celery salt and bring to boil. Reduce heat.
4. Add peanut butter and cream.
5. Heat, stirring constantly, until peanut butter is thoroughly dissolved and soup is hot.
6. Pour into hot soup bowls or mugs and garnish with generous dollop of sour cream.

Seven Minute Mushroom Surprise

Preparation time: 7 minutes   Serves 2

**1 can Cream of
Mushroom soup**

**1 soup can milk (or Half
and Half)**

**1 4 oz. can mushrooms,
drained reserving half of
liquid**

⅛ t. Accent

1 T. sherry

1 T. Parmesan cheese

1. Combine soup, milk, mushrooms, liquid from can, and Accent.
2. Bring to boil and reduce heat, stirring constantly.
3. Simmer five minutes.
4. Add sherry and Parmesan.
5. Pour into hot soup bowls.

SOUPS...ICY COLD!

Zesty Iced Tomato Soup

Preparation time: 9 minutes   Serves 4 heartily

4 cups tomato juice
1 cup lemon yogurt
½ t. salt
**½ t. coarsely ground
  black pepper**

1 t. dill seed
2 t. dried chopped chives
1 8 oz. carton Jalapeno dip
1 t. dried parsley

1. Put 2 cups tomato juice, yogurt, salt, pepper, dill seed, and chives in blender and liquefy.
2. Pour into large mixing bowl.
3. Put remaining 2 cups tomato juice, Jalapeño dip and parsley into blender and liquefy.
4. Pour into mixing bowl with other ingredients, stirring well.
5. Refrigerate until cold.
6. Garnish with fresh chopped parsley if available.

**Note: This soup can be served immediately, but the
      longer refrigerated the better the taste.**

Gaspacho Blanco

Preparation time: 11 minutes   Serves 4 heartily

2 cucumbers peeled and seeded

1 14½ oz. can Swanson's Chicken Broth

1 10¾ oz. can Cream of Potato soup

1 8 oz. carton sour cream

2 t. Tarragon vinegar

½ t. salt

green pepper, cucumber, green onion for garnish

1. Cut peeled and seeded cucumbers into chunks to make approximately 2 heaping cups.
2. Pour chicken broth into blender and add cucumbers. Blend until liquefied and pour into mixing bowl.
3. Put Cream of Potato soup, sour cream, vinegar, and salt into blender and liquefy.
4. Combine with chicken broth and cucumber mixture. Stir with wire whisk until well blended.
5. Refrigerate until cold.
6. Float minced green peppers, minced cucumbers, and minced green onions on top of each serving. Sprinkle with paprika and serve ice cold.

Chilled Cucumber Soup

Preparation time: 13 minutes   Serves 4

2 cucumbers peeled and seeded

1 14½ oz. can Swanson's Chicken Broth

1 10¾ oz. can Cream of Potato soup

1 8 oz. carton sour cream

2 t. Tarragon vinegar

½ t. salt

1. Follow directions in above recipe.
2. When all ingredients are blended together, pour through tightly meshed colander or sieve.
3. Refrigerate until cold.
4. Sprinkle each serving with paprika for color and garnish with chopped fresh parsley.

SANDWICH HEYDAY!

Super Sandwiches That Make a Hearty Meal!

SANDWICH HEYDAY!

The Gondola

(Italian version of the American submarine)

Preparation time: 15 minutes
Cooking time: 20 minutes
Serves 4 heartily

1 loaf Italian bread
1 clove garlic
1 T. olive oil (subtitutes: corn or safflower oil)
½ t. Italian Herb seasoning (or ¼ t. basil, ¼ t. oregano)
1 3 oz. package thin sliced Italian salami

½ Bermuda onion thinly sliced
½ green pepper sliced in thin strips
salt and pepper (optional)
1 4 oz. package shredded Mozzarella cheese
1 medium ripe tomato (optional)

1. Preheat oven to 450 degrees.
2. Slice top off loaf of bread and scoop out soft inside, leaving mostly crust.
3. Peel and halve garlic clove. Rub both inside and outside of loaf. Discard.
4. Sprinkle 1 T. oil over inside of loaf.
5. Sprinkle ½ t. Italian Herb seasoning over bottom and sides of loaf.
6. On bottom half of loaf, layer as follows: half the salami topped with $^1/_3$ of Mozzarella cheese; all the green pepper and onion topped with second third of Mozzarella cheese; remainder of salami and remainder of cheese.
7. Place top on bread loaf and secure with toothpicks if necessary.
8. Wrap tightly in foil and place in 450 degree oven.
9. Cook 20 minutes.
10. Let stand a minute or two before slicing.

Suggested garnish: Thin slices of tomato which can either be inserted in sandwich or eaten separately.

Pita Tropicale

(a medley of exotic fruits on whole wheat pita bread)

Preparation time: 12 minutes   Serves 4

2 ripe kiwi fruit (kee-wee)
1 ripe avocado
2 ripe papayas

4 whole wheat pita bread pockets
2 oz. fresh sprouts, washed and drained
2 T. bottled lemon juice

CHOOSING FRUIT: Papayas should be greenish yellow to almost full yellow in color and give to gentle pressure. Kiwi fruit should be as soft as a ripe pear for best eating. Avocados should give just a little bit to gentle pressure. Do not pinch as they bruise easily.

1. Cut avocado in half lengthwise and remove seed.
2. Remove skin and slice lengthwise into thin slivers. Place in bowl.
3. Peel kiwi, cut into thin slivers, and place in bowl along with avocado.
4. Slice papayas in half lengthwise; remove seeds. Slice into slivers and put into bowl with other fruit.
5. Add sprouts.
6. Toss gently with 2 T. bottled lemon juice.
7. Cut section off pita bread and fill each pocket with fruit-sprout mixture.
8. Drizzle any left over lemon juice equally into sandwiches.

PITA BREAD

Note: No dressing needed with this sandwich. Juices of fruits and oil of avocado create the perfect moisture.

California Carousel

(a riot of tasty fresh vegetables, full of protein,
and a dieter's delight!)

Preparation time: 12 minutes   Serves 2

2 oz. fresh mushrooms

½ medium size green pepper

½ medium size tomato thinly sliced

1½ T. mayonnaise (no substitutes)

4 thin slices sweet (Bermuda) onion

4 slices Munster cheese

1 cup fresh sprouts, washed and drained

2 whole wheat pita bread pockets

Heaping ⅛ t. garlic powder

1. Cut section off pita bread to make pocket as shown, p. 36.
2. Mix mayonnaise and garlic powder. Spread on inside of both pockets.
3. Chop mushrooms and green pepper into bite-sized pieces.
4. Slice tomato and onion.
5. Combine mushrooms, green pepper, and sprouts, mixing well.
6. Fill each pocket with mixture of mushrooms, peppers, and sprouts.
7. Insert slices of tomato, onion, and cheese.

Suggested garnish: Ripe olives and a lemon wedge.

Scandinavian Hero

(ham, Provalone cheese, and green pepper)

Preparation time: 10 minutes   Serves 4

½ lb. thinly sliced ham
1 green pepper sliced in
thin strips
1 6 oz. package thin sliced
Provalone cheese
mayonnaise (no
substitutes)

Dijon mustard
lettuce
8 slices rye bread

1. Spread half bread slices liberally with mayonnaise, half with mustard.
2. Layer equal amounts of ham, cheese, green pepper and lettuce on 4 slices, topping with remaining bread.

Jet Age Reuben

Preparation time: 10 minutes   Serves 4

1 8 oz. can sauerkraut,
drained
½ lb. thinly sliced corned
beef
1 6 oz. package sliced
Swiss cheese
butter or margarine

2 t. caraway seeds
8 slices rye bread
Durkee or Thousand
Island dressing

1. Spread each bread slice with Durkee or Thousand Island dressing.
2. Layer corned beef, cheese, and sauerkraut on 4 bottom bread slices.
3. Sprinkle each with ½ t. caraway seeds.
4. Top with remaining bread slices.
5. Spread each side of sandwich lightly with butter and grill until cheese is melted and sandwich is hot throughout.

Suggested garnish: chips and pickles.

Deviled Ham Reuben

Preparation time: 6 minutes   Serves 2

**1 6 oz. package sliced
  Munster cheese**
1 4½ oz. can deviled ham
4 slices rye bread

Dijon mustard
¼ cup sauerkraut, drained
butter

1. Spread bread slices with liberal amount of mustard.
2. Cut half of cheese to fit on 2 bread slices.
3. Spread with deviled ham and top with sauerkraut, rest of cheese, and bread.
4. Lightly butter both sides of sandwich and grill until cheese is melted.

Suggested garnish: Stuffed green olives and radishes in lettuce cup.

The Cape Cod

(smoked salmon and cream cheese)

Preparation time: 10 minutes   Serves 4

**1 6½ oz. can smoked
salmon, drained**
**1 3 oz. package cream
cheese, softened**
**1 T. mayonnaise (no
substitutes)**
⅓ cup fresh minced onions
¼ t. pepper

¼ t. salt
⅓ cup ripe olives sliced
4 crisp lettuce leaves
**8 slices rye bread
(or bagels)**

1. Combine cream cheese, onions, olives, salt, pepper and mayonnaise.
2. Beat by hand until well mixed and smooth.
3. Spread mixture on 4 bread slices, top with salmon, lettuce and remaining bread.

Suggested garnish: Fresh fruit or canned and chilled peach half.

Texas Barbecue

(hot barbecued beef or pork for the robust appetite)

Preparation time: 5 minutes   Cooking time: 10 minutes
Serves 4 (based on ⅛ lb. per person)

**½ lb. thinly sliced beef or
pork bought from local
delicatessen**

1 bottle barbecue sauce
4 sesame seed buns

1. Preheat oven to 350 degrees.
2. Put beef or pork in pan and pour enough barbecue sauce over it to cover.
3. Simmer for 10 minutes.

4. Pop buns in oven to warm.
5. Put equal amounts of beef into each bun and top with generous portion of barbecue sauce.
6. Serve piping hot.

Suggested garnish: Delicatessen coleslaw and dill pickle spear.

The Egg

(egg salad sandwich done a little differently)

Preparation time: 12 minutes   Serves 4

See rule for hard-cooked eggs, p. 238.

4 hard-cooked eggs
2 T. mayonnaise (no substitutes)
2 T. Dijon mustard
scant ¼ t. celery seed (optional)
Additional mayonnaise for bread slices

¼ t. salt
⅛ t. pepper
1 pinch sugar (optional)
8 slices bread (rye or French
4 crisp lettuce leaves

1. Remove shells from eggs and chop.
2. Combine mayonnaise, mustard, salt, pepper, celery seed, and sugar with eggs until well mixed.
3. Spread additional mayonnaise on all bread slices.
4. Divide egg mixture evenly among 4 bread slices.
5. Top with crisp lettuce leaf and remaining bread slices.

Suggested garnish: Sweet pickles and chips.

The Basic Tuna

Preparation time: 10 minutes
Serves 4 (or 2 as a salad)

1 7 oz. can white tuna, drained

¼ cup mayonnaise (no substitutes)

2 T. sweet pickle relish (or equivalent amount of chopped sweet pickle plus a little juice)

8 slices toasted French bread

4 crisp lettuce leaves

¼ t. salt

½ t. celery seed (optional)

1. Pop bread under broiler to brown.
2. Mix tuna, mayonnaise, pickle relish, salt and celery seed together.
3. Spread on toasted French bread and top with a crisp lettuce leaf and remaining bread half.

Suggested garnish: Fresh tomato, if possible, or chips and green olives.

Toasted Tuna Special

Preparation time: 10 minutes   Cooking time: 15-20 minutes
Serves 4

1 7 oz. can tuna, drained

½ T. instant minced onion

1 t. celery seed

½ t. salt

¼ t. pepper

¼ cup mayonnaise (no substitutes)

¼ cup finely chopped sweet pickle

8 slices American cheese

4 hamburger buns, split and lightly buttered

1. Preheat oven to 350 degrees.
2. Mix together: tuna, celery seed, minced onion, salt, pepper, mayonnaise and pickle.
3. Place 1 slice of cheese on bottom halves of buns.
4. Add tuna mixture, remaining cheese slices, and top half of bun.
5. Wrap each sandwich in aluminum foil, edges folded securely.
6. Bake 350 degrees until cheese is melted and sandwich is hot throughout. (Approximately 15-20 minutes)

Suggested garnish: Potato chips and slice of canned pineapple.

Asparagus Rolls

Preparation time: 10 minutes   Serves 4

1 16 oz. can asparagus spears, drained

8 slices white sandwich bread

mayonnaise (no substitutes)

salt and pepper

1. Cut crusts from bread and roll each slice with rolling pin until flattened.
2. Cover each slice with generous amount of mayonnaise.
3. Place drained asparagus spear in middle of each slice.
4. Sprinkle with salt and pepper and make into a roll.
5. Secure with a toothpick and sprinkle lightly with paprika for color.

Suggested garnish: Fresh fruit cup.

The Diplomat

(tuna, ripe olives, tomatoes served open-faced on English muffins)

Preparation time: 10-12 minutes   Cooking time: 5 minutes

Serves 4

2 English muffins, split and buttered

1 7 oz. can tuna, drained

4 slices of tomato

2 medium stalks celery chopped

¼ cup pitted ripe olives sliced

½ cup mayonnaise (no substitutes)

¼ t. salt

⅛ t. pepper

4 slices Velveeta

1. Run English muffins under broiler until lightly browned.
2. Mix tuna, celery, olives, salt, pepper, and mayonnaise together.
3. Place one tomato slice on each muffin.
4. Spread tuna mixture over tomato slices.
5. Top each muffin with 1 slice of cheese.
6. Run under broiler until cheese is melted.

Suggested garnish: Sprig of parsley on top of each sandwich and hard-cooked eggs sliced lengthwise to side.

The International

(hotdogs, cheese, and bacon)

Preparation time: 10 minutes   Cooking time: 10 minutes
Serves 2

4 frankfurters

4 buns

4 slices bacon

mustard

¼ cup minced onion (fresh)

4 thin slices cheese or ½ cup grated sharp cheese

1. Split each frankfurter lengthwise, but not cutting all the way through.
2. Chop onion finely and sprinkle in slits of frankfurters.
3. Tear cheese in bite-sized pieces and add to onion.
4. Wrap each frankfurter with 1 bacon slice and secure with toothpick.
5. Place under broiler about 5″ from heat and cook until bacon is crisp.
6. Turn and cook other side.
7. Spread buns with mustard. Place frankfurters inside buns and warm in oven.

Suggested garnish: Potato chips.

Tyrolean Poorboy

(salami, pastrami, cream cheese, horseradish on rye)

Preparation time: 10 minutes   Serves 4

1 3 oz. package cream cheese, softened
½ T. milk
½ t. hot horseradish
½ Bermuda onion thinly sliced

½ lb. thinly sliced salami and pastrami (or may substitute deli corned beef, roast beef, etc.)
8 slices dark rye bread

1. Combine cream cheese, horseradish, and milk. Mix until smooth.
2. Spread cream cheese mixture evenly on all 8 slices of bread.
3. Divide meat into 4 servings and place on 4 slices of bread.
4. Top with thinly sliced onions and remaining bread.

Suggested garnish: Dill pickle spears and sweet cherry peppers.

CAMARADERIE THROUGH FOOD
LET THE GUESTS DO THE WORK!!!

CAMARADERIE THROUGH FOOD
LET THE GUESTS DO THE WORK!!!

Fondue Bourguignonne
Sauce Accompaniments:
Bearnaise.............Horseradish
Mild Curry...Hot Mexican
Bibb Lettuce with Oil and Vinegar
Hot French Bread
Cherry Pecan Parfait

Cheese Fondue à la Lucerne
Toasted Cubes of French Bread
Spinach Salad with Tarragon Egg Dressing
Strawberry Angel

Tacos 'Ole Mexico
Condiments
Dill Pickles
Ice Cream Sandwiches
Mexican Coffee

Festive Gypsy Salad Bar
Assortment of Cheese and Crackers
Dessert

This best of parties can be the easiest! Nothing more fun for long winter evenings than surprising guests with a fondue feast—the Bourguignonne or the classic Swiss.

Gathering around the fondue pot, spearing a cube of bread or meat, and dipping deeply into a bubbling mixture reflects the ancient belief that eating out of the same dish creates an atmosphere of intimacy and togetherness. Penalties when dippers lose food add to the gaiety—buy a bottle of wine or kiss the person next to you!

(A substitute for a fondue pot can be an electric frying pan, a chafing dish, or heat-proof dish that fits over an alcohol burner or canned heat. No fondue forks? Use wooden or bamboo skewers available everywhere.)

Menu I

Fondue Bourguignonne

Sauce Accompaniments:

Bearnaise. . . Horseradish

Mild Curry. . . Hot Mexican

Bibb Lettuce with Oil and Vinegar

Hot French Bread

Red Wine

Cherry Pecan Parfait

Coffee

Fondue Bourguignonne

Preparation time: only the minutes it takes to set up the table
Serves 4

2 lbs. beef tenderloin   **1 t. salt**
cubed*
3 cups peanut or corn oil

*Beef tenderloin is expensive, but the most economical
because of no bone and no waste. Allow half-pound meat
per person.

1. Have butcher cut meat into 1½ - 2 inch cubes.

2. Put meat on tray with fondue pot.
3. Pour oil into pot and add salt.
4. Heat oil until hot enough to cook meat cubes in 15 to 50
seconds.

Bearnaise Sauce *

Preparation time: 11 minutes   Makes 1 cup

Part I

2 T. chicken broth
2 T. tarragon vinegar

¾ t. bottled lemon juice
**3 T. chopped green onions
(tops included)**

Part II

3 egg yolks
**½ cup butter (1 stick),
  softened**
2 sprays celery leaves
2 sprigs parsley

½ t. salt
**⅛ t. coarsely ground black
  pepper**
¼ t. Tabasco

1. Bring all ingredients in Part I to a boil.
2. Place all ingredients in Part II in blender and run at medium speed.
3. Slowly pour hot mixture (Part I) into blender while running. Mix well.
4. Cook over hot water until sauce thickens — about 3-4 minutes, stirring constantly.

* If serving only one sauce, serve Bearnaise — it is excellent.

Note: Will keep a week or two in refrigerator. Also freezes well. If frozen, do not cook to thicken until ready to use.

Horseradish Sauce

Preparation time: 5 minutes   Makes 1 heaping cup

1 8 oz. carton sour cream   **½ t. dry mustard**
3 T. horseradish   **¼ t. bottled lemon juice**
2 T. Durkee dressing

1. Mix all ingredients together until well combined.
2. Place in serving bowl and refrigerate until ready to use.
3. Let come to room temperature before using.

Note: Keeps well for a week or two. Also freezes well.

Mild Curry Sauce

Preparation time: 13 minutes   Makes 1½ cups

¾ t. instant chicken   **½ t. salt**
** bouillon**   **¾ t. sugar**
½ cup boiling water   **⅛ t. powdered ginger**
2½ T. butter   **1 t. curry powder**
3 T. flour   **¾ t. bottled lemon juice**
1 cup milk
¾ t. minced dried onion

1. Dissolve bouillon in ½ cup boiling water.
2. Melt butter in saucepan and blend in flour.
3. Slowly add milk and minced onion, stirring until smooth.
4. Add salt, sugar, ginger, curry, and lemon juice.
5. Stir until sauce is smooth and thickened.

Note: Keeps well for a week. Can be frozen.

Hot Mexican Sauce

Preparation time: 7 minutes   Makes 1½ cups

2 t. beef bouillon granules
½ cup boiling water
2 whole canned hot chili peppers
2 t. chopped mild green chili peppers (plus juice)

1 8 oz. can tomato sauce
½ t. garlic powder
Very scant ⅛ t. sugar

1. Dissolve bouillon granules in ½ cup boiling water.
2. Split hot chili peppers lengthwise and remove seeds with thumb.
3. Put all ingredients in blender and blend until thoroughly mixed.
4. Serve at room temperature.

Note: Keeps well for a week or two. Can be frozen.

Bibb Lettuce with Oil and Vinegar

Preparation time: 10 minutes   Serves 4

1 head Bibb lettuce
1 package Good Seasons Oil and Vinegar Salad Dressing Mix

¼ cup red wine vinegar
2 T. water
⅔ cup oil (olive oil preferred)

1. Wash and drain lettuce well.
2. Dry on paper towels and refrigerate in air tight bag until ready to use.
3. Combine salad dressing mix, vinegar, water, and oil. Shake until well mixed.
4. Tear lettuce into bite sized pieces and toss lightly with dressing.

Hot French Bread

Preparation time: 10 minutes   Serves 6-8

1 loaf bakery French bread   ½ stick butter

1. Cut loaf of bread lengthwise from end to end. Do not cut all the way through.
2. Cut crosswise in 1" slices, again, not cutting all the way through.
3. Butter each slice well.
4. Heat in 350 degree oven 10-12 minutes until nicely browned and crisp.

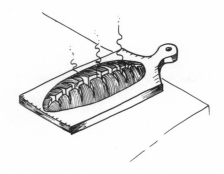

Cherry Pecan Parfait

Preparation time: 6 minutes   Serves 4

4 cups Ranch or Butter   1 16 oz. can pitted Bing
Pecan ice cream   cherries

1. Divide ice cream evenly among four dessert dishes or parfait glasses.
2. Cover with foil and place in freezer until ready to use.
3. 10 minutes before serving time, remove from freezer and pour cherries with a little juice over each serving.

Menu II

Cheese Fondue á la Lucerne

Toasted Cubes of French Bread

Spinach Salad with Tarragon Egg Dressing

White Wine

Strawberry Angel

Coffee

Cheese Fondue á la Lucerne

Preparation time: 12-15 minutes   Serves 4

1 garlic clove crushed
2 cups dry white wine
2 cups grated Gruyére or Monterey Jack cheese
2 cups grated natural Swiss cheese
2 T. cornstarch

4 T. Kirschwasser
⅛ t. cayenne pepper or Tabasco
¼ t. salt
scant ⅛ t. nutmeg (optional)

1. Rub fondue pot or cooking container with garlic clove and discard.
2. Put wine into pot and heat until simmering.
3. Mix together cornstarch and Kirschwasser. Set aside.
4. Add cheese to fondue pot slowly, stirring occasionally as cheese melts. (CAUTION: Do not overheat or cheese will become stringy.)
5. Add Kirschwasser to fondue, stirring constantly until thickened.
6. Add cayenne, salt, and optional nutmeg. Taste and correct seasoning.

Note: Instruct guests to spear a cube of bread and dip deeply into the pot with a swirling motion. This insures ample coating of bread cube and prevents separation of fondue.

Toasted Cubes of French Bread

Preparation time: 5 minutes   Serves 6-8

1 loaf French or Italian bread

1. Preheat oven to 300 degrees.
2. Cut loaf into bite sized cubes and place on cookie sheet.
3. Toast in 300 degree oven until crisp and lightly brown—
   8-10 minutes.
4. Heap toasted cubes around fondue pot and let guests
   help themselves.

Note: Make ahead, store in air-tight container.

Spinach Salad

Serves 4

1 pound fresh spinach   2 green onions minced

1. Wash spinach, drain well, tear into bite sized pieces.
2. Chop fine 2 green onions—include tops.
3. Refrigerate in air-tight plastic bag until ready for use.
4. At serving time place spinach and onions in large salad
   bowl and toss well.
5. Top each serving with egg dressing.

Tarragon Egg Dressing

(can be made 3-4 days ahead)

(see rule for hard-cooked eggs p. 238)

Makes 1 cup

3 hard-boiled eggs peeled	**½ cup sour cream**
1 T. prepared horseradish	**¼ cup mayonnaise**
1½ t. tarragon vinegar	**¼ t. Tabasco**
1 t. Dijon mustard	**¼ t. each salt and pepper**

1. Chop fine or grate eggs.
2. Combine with all other ingredients.
3. Serve over fresh spinach.
4. Can substitute Good Seasons Italian Salad Dressing mix.

Strawberry Angel

Preparation time: 15 minutes   Serves 6-8

1 bakery angel food cake (8-10 oz.)	**1 pint vanilla ice cream**
2 10 oz. packages cut up frozen strawberries, thawed and drained	**1 carton whipped topping with real cream**
1 10 oz. package whole frozen strawberries, thawed and drained	

1. Split angel food cake in half crosswise.
2. Cover bottom half with one half of ice cream and 1 10 oz. package thawed cut up strawberries.
3. Put other half on top of cake and spread with remaining ice cream and cut up strawberries.
4. Place in freezer until ice cream is firm.
5. Remove from freezer and ice with whipped topping and decorate with whole strawberries.
6. Wrap in foil, sealing edges, and return to freezer until approximately 15 minutes before serving.
7. Serve whole or in wedges.

Menu III

Tacos 'Ole Mexico

Condiments

Dill Pickles

Ice Cream Sandwiches

Mexican Coffee

This one dish meal, an all generation hit, can be cooked and served from the kitchen counter in the same gaily decorated pot. A tall bountiful bouquet of brightly colored napkins, matching paper plates, and colored paper condiment bowls carry out a fiesta-like party theme.

Tacos 'Ole Mexico

Preparation and Cooking time: 30 minutes
Serves 4-6 (depending upon appetites)

2 lbs. lean hamburger meat **1 medium onion**

2 8 oz. cans tomato sauce **1 jar hot Taco sauce**

2 packages Taco seasoning **1-2 packages Taco shells**

1 T. dried minced onion **½ head Iceberg lettuce**

1 t. Taco spice **1 tomato**

1 small can minced mild **1 jar dill pickles chilled**
green chili peppers

1 8 oz. package grated
sharp Cheddar cheese

1. Place meat in pan and brown over moderate heat.
2. Drain thoroughly and return to pan.
3. Add to meat: tomato sauce, Taco seasoning, minced onion, Taco spice.
4. Stir well to combine ingredients.
5. Cover and bring to a boil. Reduce heat to simmer.
6. Cook 15 minutes, stirring occasionally.
7. While meat is cooking, prepare condiments and place each in individual bowls.
   Drain chili peppers
   Put cheese and Taco sauce in individual
       condiment bowls.
   Chop onion fine
   Chop half head of lettuce
   Mince one tomato and drain on paper towel
   Slice dill pickles and place in bowl to side
8. Pop Taco shells in preheated 350 degree oven for 5 minutes just before serving.

Note: Guests preferring taco salads can break up taco shells and spoon sauce and condiments over them.

Ice Cream Sandwiches

(buy at the grocery and keep in freezer until ready to serve)

Mexican Coffee

Preparation time: 5 minutes   Serves 4

4 cups water
4 T. instant coffee
½ cup dark brown sugar

⅛ t. ground cinnamon
4 whole cloves

1. Combine water, coffee, sugar, cinnamon, and cloves in saucepan.
2. Bring to a boil, stirring until sugar is dissolved.
3. Reduce heat and simmer 10 minutes.
4. Serve piping hot.

Note: Can be made a day in advance and reheated. Freezes well.

Menu IV
Festive Gypsy Salad Bar

Salad Greens and Accompaniments

Tempting Dressings. . . Store Bought

Bleu Cheese, Oil and Vinegar, Thousand Island,

Creamy Cucumber

Assortment of Cheese

Edam. . .Munster. . .Sharp Cheddar. . .Roquefort

Crackers

Iced Beer and Soft Drinks

A Pie?. . .Cookies?. . .A Cake?

Coffee

HELP YOURSELF TO A FESTIVE GYPSY SALAD BUFFET
STRAIGHT FROM THE COOK'S COUNTER!

On the Counter:

Colorful and durable dinner size paper plates and
matching napkins
Salad forks and teaspoons
Serving forks and spoons
Earthenware or paper bowls for salad accompaniments
Large glass bowl or tray of chilled, crisp and torn greens
for salad base
An inviting variety of bottled salad dressings
An assortment of cheese and crackers
Dessert
A pot of coffee
(and close by—a tub of iced beer and soft drinks)

Festive Gypsy Salad Bar

Preparation time: determined by variety and quantity offered
Serves 8-10

1 head Boston or Bibb lettuce

1 bunch Romaine lettuce

1 head Iceberg lettuce

½ lb. salami cut in bite sized pieces*

½ lb. thin ham slivers*

½ lb. thin turkey strips*

2 diced green peppers

1 head cauliflower (flowerettes only)

1 head fresh broccoli (flowerettes only)

½ lb. fresh mushrooms sliced

2 thinly sliced raw zucchini or yellow squash

½ lb. fresh bean sprouts

1 16 oz. can ripe seedless olives

1 box salad croutons

1 jar bacon bits

2 cucumbers seeded and diced

2 bunches green onions diced

1 16 oz. can chi chi beans

2 hard-cooked eggs chopped

* Choose a minimum of two

1. Wash lettuce and drain well. If preparing the night before, wrap each washed and well-drained head in paper toweling and refrigerate in air-tight plastic bag.
2. When ready to use, tear into approximately 2½ to 3½ inch pieces and place in large glass bowls.
3. Wash all vegetables and drain well.
4. Slice or dice into bite sized pieces.
5. Place in individual serving containers and cover tightly. Refrigerate.

Note: Keep all salad greens and accompaniments well chilled until party time.

Assortment of Cheese and Crackers

1 7 oz. round of Edam

**1 8 oz. square sharp
Cheddar**

1 10 oz. rectangle Munster

1 6 oz. round Bleu

**Saltines, Wheat Thins and
Triscuits — 1 box each**

Decorate tray with parsley

* These are only suggestions and estimated amounts for
8 guests.

Dessert

The grand finale can be the effortless selection of irresistible
desserts from the grocery frozen food section.

JUST THE TWO OF US

30-Minute Dinners with a Flair!

JUST THE TWO OF US

Note: To add a quick dessert, see Dessert chapter, p. 213

Menu I

Salmon Royale

Grilled Tomatoes Italiante

Green Peas with Chives

Watermelon Rind Pickles

Bread (optional)

Coffee. . .Hot Tea

Salmon Royale

Preparation time: 15 minutes   Cooking time: 10 minutes
Serves 2 heartily

1 7¾ oz. can red salmon	**¾ cup grated Swiss cheese**
½ cup cracker crumbs	**Scant ⅛ t. nutmeg**
1 egg	**¼ t. salt**
½ cup dry white wine	**1 T. butter**

1. Preheat oven to 200 degrees and heat plates.
2. Drain salmon and reserve liquid. (Set liquid aside for salmon sauce.)
3. Flake salmon, removing any bones.
4. Combine salmon, cracker crumbs, egg, wine, cheese, nutmeg, and salt. Mix well.
5. Form into 4 medium sized patties.
6. Melt 1 T. butter in skillet and cook over medium heat until just slightly brown.
7. Sauté patties in melted butter until done — about 5 minutes each side.
8. Serve with salmon sauce (see next page) and garnish with parsley.

Salmon Royale Sauce

½ cup milk
½ T. cornstarch dissolved
  in 2 T. milk (take 2 T.
  from ½ cup)
liquid from salmon

1 T. bottled lemon juice
  plus ½ t.
½ T. dried minced parsley
1 t. butter
1 egg yolk

1. While salmon patties are cooking, heat milk and cornstarch in salmon liquid.
2. Add lemon juice, parsley, butter, and egg yolk.
3. Stir constantly until thickened—about 5 minutes.
4. Spoon over patties and sprinkle lightly with paprika for color. Garnish with parsley.

Grilled Tomatoes Italiante

Preparation time: 5 minutes   Cooking time: 10 minutes
Serves 2

1 large firm ripe tomato
1 T. butter or margarine,
  melted
⅛ t. (scant) Italian herbs

scant ⅛ t. black pepper
1 t. grated Parmesan
  cheese

1. Preheat oven to 350 degrees.
2. Halve tomato crosswise.
3. Place in shallow baking dish and brush with melted butter. (Or rub lightly with cooking or olive oil.)
4. Sprinkle scant ⅛ t. Italian Herbs on tomato halves and top with pepper and cheese.
5. Bake 350 degrees for 10 minutes—until tomatoes are medium soft, but not mushy.

Green Peas with Chives

Preparation and Cooking time: 10 minutes
Serves 2 with ample leftovers for seconds

**1 10 oz. box frozen
green peas**

**½ t. chopped dried chives
1 T. butter**

1. Cook peas according to directions with ½ t. chives.
   DO NOT OVERCOOK!
2. Drain and toss with 1 T. butter.

Watermelon Rind Pickles

1 6-8 oz. jar watermelon rind pickles, chilled

1. Place in freezer to chill if not already cold.
2. Drain and place in small serving bowl as accompaniment
   to dinner.

Menu II

Chicken Breasts Supreme

Herbed Rice

Purple Plum Pineapple Salad

Lemon-Honey Dressing

Coffee or Hot Tea

Chicken Breasts Supreme

Preparation and Cooking time: 30 minutes   Serves 2

2 chicken breasts
salt and pepper
1½ T. margarine
¼ t. Tabasco
1 10¾ oz. Cream of Mushroom soup

¼ cup milk
¾ cup grated sharp Cheddar cheese
scant ¼ t. salt
1 2 oz. can mushrooms, drained (optional)

1. Melt margarine in skillet or electric frying pan over medium heat.
2. Sprinkle chicken breasts lightly with salt and pepper.
3. Lightly brown chicken breasts in hot margarine, turning after one side is brown. (About 6 minutes each side.)
4. While chicken is browning, mix together Tabasco, soup, milk, cheese, salt and drained mushrooms.
5. When chicken is browned, pour off all but 1 T. of remaining margarine in skillet and add soup mixture.
6. Cover and simmer for 15 minutes, basting occasionally.
7. Heat plates in a 200 degree oven while chicken is cooking.
8. To serve: Place one chicken breast on each plate, spoon sauce over each piece, sprinkle with paprika and garnish with parsley.
   Pass remaining sauce in a pitcher or gravy boat.

Note: To double Chicken Breasts Supreme use: 4 chicken breasts, 3 T. margarine or butter, 5–6 drops Tabasco, 1 10¾ oz. can Cream Mushroom soup, ½ cup milk, 1 cup grated sharp Cheddar cheese, ½ t. salt, and 1 4 oz. can mushrooms, drained.

Herbed Rice

Preparation time: 15 minutes   Serves 4 (remainder freezes well)

1 box Golden Grain Chicken Flavor Rice-A-Roni
2 T. butter or margarine

2¾ cups hot water
1 Flavor Packet (inside box)

(Brown rice when Step 4 of Chicken Breasts Supreme is completed)

1. In frying pan, brown rice mixture in 2 T. butter until light brown. Stir frequently so as not to burn.
2. Pour hot water into rice mixture and stir in Flavor Packet.
3. Cover pan and simmer until liquid is absorbed and rice tender.

Purple Plum Pineapple salad

Preparation time: 5 minutes   Serves 2

**1 7 oz. can pineapple
slices, drained, reserving
¼ cup juice**

**1 7 oz. can purple plums,
drained**

1. Put drained pineapple and plums in freezer to chill if not
   already refrigerated. About 10 minutes.
2. Place on bed of lettuce and dribble lemon-honey dressing
   over fruit.
3. Sprinkle lightly with paprika for color.

Lemon-Honey Dressing

Preparation time: 5 minutes   Makes ½ cup

**¼ cup honey
¼ cup pineapple juice
   reserved from drained
   pineapple**

1 t. bottled lemon juice

1. Mix together honey, pineapple juice, and lemon juice.
2. Stir until well mixed.
3. Dribble dressing over chilled fruit.

Menu III

Ham and Asparagus with Mustard Sauce

Spinach Cassini

Spiced Peaches

Hot Bread (optional)

Coffee or Hot Tea

Ham and Asparagus with Mustard Sauce

Preparation time: 15 minutes
Cooking time: 10 minutes or less   Serves 2

1 15 oz. can green asparagus spears
¼-⅓ lb. fully cooked and deboned ham slices, ⅛-¼ inches thick
2 T. flour
2 T. butter

½ cup asparagus liquid
½ cup milk
¼ t. salt
1 t. bottled lemon juice
2 t. Dijon mustard

1. Preheat oven to 350 degrees.
2. Drain asparagus spears, reserving liquid.
3. Lay ham slices in small casserole dish.
4. Place 4 to 5 asparagus spears over each ham slice or divide whole can equally.
5. In saucepan melt butter, adding ½ cup asparagus liquid.
6. Stir in flour.
7. Add milk, salt, lemon juice, and mustard, blending until smooth.
8. Bring sauce to rolling boil, stirring constantly.
9. Reduce heat, continue cooking until mixture has thickened — about 10 minutes.
10. Spoon sauce over asparagus and ham in casserole.
11. Place in oven and cook approximately 8-10 minutes — only until hot.

Spinach Cassini

Preparation time: 10 minutes   Cooking time: 20 minutes
Serves 2 heartily

**1 10 oz. package frozen
chopped spinach, thawed**
**1 3 oz. package cream
cheese, softened**
1½ t. dried chopped chives
**¼ t. coarsely ground black
pepper**

1 t. salt
¼ cup bread crumbs
½ T. butter
Paprika

1. Preheat oven to 350 degrees.
2. Squeeze water out of spinach.
3. Blend spinach, cream cheese, chives, pepper, and salt
   either by hand, mixer, or food processor.
4. Spoon into lightly buttered small casserole.
5. Top with bread crumbs and dot with ½ T. butter.
6. Cook 20 minutes at 350°—run under broiler last 2
   minutes to brown lightly.
7. Sprinkle with paprika and divide into 2 serving portions.

Spiced Peaches

Place can of spiced peaches in freezer to chill while dinner
is being prepared. Drain, pat dry, and place on plate when
everything else is ready.

Menu IV

Mexican Nacho Cheese Bake

Corn Relish

Avocado Strips and Tomato Wedge Salad

with

Oil and Vinegar Dressing

Corn Sticks (optional)

Coffee or Hot Tea

Mexican Nacho Cheese Bake

Preparation and Cooking time: 25 minutes   Serves 2 heartily

½ **lb. lean ground hamburger meat**
½ **T. dried minced onion**
1 package Taco seasoning
1 8 oz. can tomato sauce

¾ **cup green chili dip**
1 4 oz. package grated sharp Cheddar cheese
2 heaping cups nacho cheese flavored Doritos

1. Preheat oven to 350 degrees.
2. Brown meat and onion in pan with lid on. Stir occasionally. About 5 minutes.
3. Drain thoroughly and return to pan.
4. Add to meat and onion mixture: 1 package Taco seasoning and 1 8 oz. can tomato sauce. Stir to mix well.
5. Let meat sauce come to a boil, reduce heat and cook over medium high for 5 minutes. Stir constantly. Remove from heat and set aside.
6. Lightly butter a small casserole or shallow pie pan.
7. Layer as follows: 1 cup Doritos coarsely crumbled on bottom of casserole, half of meat sauce, half of green chili dip, half of grated cheese. Repeat layers.
8. Bake 350 degrees for 10 minutes. Let set 2 minutes before serving.
9. For added crunchiness, sprinkle additional Doritos on top.

Corn Relish

1 small jar Mexican corn relish, chilled

1. Pop corn relish in freezer to chill if not refrigerated in advance.
2. Drain and serve.

Avocado Strips and Tomato Wedge Salad

Preparation time: 10 minutes   Serves 2

1 ripe avocado   **1 ripe tomato**

1. Cut avocado in half lengthwise and remove seed.
2. Peel skin by holding avocado cut side down in palm of hand. Begin at top and peel away skin.
3. Cut in lengthwise, uniform slices.
4. Quarter tomato and slice in half again.
5. Place tomato wedges and avocado slices on bed of crisp lettuce and sprinkle lightly with oil and vinegar dressing.

Oil and Vinegar Dressing

Preparation time: 3 minutes   Makes 1 cup

¼ cup red wine vinegar   **⅔ cup olive oil**
2 T. water   **1 package Good Seasons Italian Salad Dressing Mix**

1. Mix all ingredients together in a bottle.
2. Shake until well blended.

Corn Sticks

Buy a box of prepared mix and follow the directions.
Serve hot with butter.

Menu V

Filet of Fish Parmesan

Broccoli with Lemon Butter

Potato Puff

Chilled Pears with Mint Jelly

Coffee or Hot Tea

A note on fish: Frozen fish should preferably be thawed before cooking, but can be cooked while still frozen. Fish cooks very quickly and overcooking will destroy the delicate flavor. Cooking time will vary according to size and thickness. To test for doneness, stick a fork or toothpick into the thickest part of the fish — if it flakes (breaks apart easily), it is ready to serve.

Filet of Fish Parmesan

Preparation time: 4 minutes   Cooking time: 10-15 minutes
Serves 2

1 lb. (fresh or frozen) boneless fish filets (any mild tasting fish— flounder, crappie, sole, trout)
3 T. butter
1 T. bottled lemon juice
1 T. dry white wine

½ t. salt
½ t. coarsely ground black pepper
¼ cup Parmesan cheese
paprika
lemon wedges

1. Preheat oven to 400 degrees.
2. Cut 3 T. butter into small cubes and place in shallow baking dish in 400 degree oven.
3. While butter is melting, sprinkle filets on both sides with ½ t. salt and ½ t. pepper.
4. Remove melted butter from oven and add lemon juice.
5. Place filets flesh side down in sizzling butter and bake in oven 10 minutes. (if fish is thick, cook 15 minutes)
6. Turn with spatula and baste with juices. Add 1 T. wine, ¼ cup Parmesan, and sprinkle with paprika.
7. Return to oven and bake until done—approximately 5 minutes.
8. To serve: garnish with parsley and lemon wedges.

Note: You may run fish under broiler if filets are not brown enough.

Broccoli with Lemon Butter

Preparation time: 2 minutes   Cooking time: 18 minutes
Serves 2 heartily

1 10 oz. package frozen   **2 t. bottled lemon juice**
broccoli spears in butter
sauce (Green Giant
preferred)

1. Put uncovered quart size saucepan of water on to boil.
2. Place unopened pouch in boiling water.
3. Cook until tender crisp—about 18 minutes.
4. Open pouch, pour into a bowl and add 2 t. bottled lemon juice.
5. Toss broccoli, butter, and lemon juice gently until broccoli is coated with sauce.

Potato Puff

Preparation and cooking time: 10 minutes
Serves 2 (with ample for seconds)

¾ cup water   **1½ T. butter**
¾ cup milk   **⅓ cup instant mashed**
¼ t. salt   **potatoes (French's)**
⅛ t. coarsely ground black   **¼ cup grated sharp**
pepper   **Cheddar cheese**
½ t. dried parsley flakes

1. Place water, milk, salt, pepper, parsley flakes, and butter in saucepan.
2. Bring to a boil.
3. Stir in instant potatoes and cheese.
4. Whip vigorously with fork or whisk until cheese. is melted and potatoes are fluffy.

Note: Will hold for an hour or two in pan, off heat. Add a dash more milk when reheating to bring back consistency.

Chilled Pears with Mint Jelly

Preparation time: 4 minutes   Serves 2

1 15½ oz. can pear halves,   1 small jar mint jelly
chilled (for flavor buy
larger size can)

1. Drain 4 pear halves and pat dry with paper towel.
2. Place on 2 small salad plates.
3. Spoon 1 t. mint jelly into each pear half.

VIP GUESTS COME TO DINNER

Impressively Elegant In 60 Minutes

VIP GUESTS COME TO DINNER

Carolina Deviled Crab
Broiled Parmesan Zucchini Halves
Bloody Mary Aspic Salad
Hot Poppy Seed Rolls
French Chocolate Pie

Brandied Filet de Boeuf
French Green Beans with Slivered Almonds
Ruby Red Raspberry Salad
Toast Halves of Pepperidge Farm Rolls
Café St. Jacques

Louisiana Shrimp Curry over Rice
condiments of:
Chutney . . . Peanuts . . . Raisins
Coconut . . . Bacon . . . Green Onions
Slivered Hard-Cooked Eggs
Cold Pineapple Bits
French Bread
Crème de Menthe over Lime Sherbet

Oriental Stir-Fried Oyster Beef
Rice
Green Cherry and Pineapple Salad
Orange Sherbet . . . Chinese Fortune Cookies

Chicken Camille
Long Grain and Wild Rice
Artichoke Hearts
Bing Cherry Salad
Orange Chiffon Surprise

Menu I

Carolina Deviled Crab

Broiled Parmesan Zucchini Halves

Bloody Mary Aspic Salad

with

Sour Cream Dressing

Hot Poppy Seed Rolls (optional)

White Wine

French Chocolate Pie

Coffee

Carolina Deviled Crab

Guaranteed to be delicious! Baked in any kind of oven-proof dish, this treasured family recipe, a deep South favorite, becomes a conversation piece when served in its natural habitat, a crab shell! (A good investment which lasts for years, crab shells are inexpensive and have a multitude of uses.)

Preparation time: 20 minutes   Cooking time: 20 minutes
Serves 6

1 lb. crab meat
*4 hard-cooked eggs,
 peeled and finely chopped
1 t. Dijon mustard
½ t. salt
½ t. Tabasco

1½ T. bottled lemon juice
1 8 oz. carton sour cream
2 T. softened butter
1 cup Saltine cracker
 crumbs
2 T. butter for top of
 mixture

1. Preheat oven to 350 degrees.
2. Remove carefully any shells from crab meat.
3. Place in large mixing bowl: crab meat, chopped eggs, mustard, salt, Tabasco, lemon juice, sour cream, and 2 T. butter.
4. Mix thoroughly and place in crab shells, ramekins, or baking dish.
5. Sprinkle cracker crumbs over top and dot with 2 T. butter divided among the 6 shells.
6. Bake 350 degrees approximately 20 minutes or until crumbs are brown on top and crab is hot throughout. DO NOT OVERCOOK!

* See rule for hard-cooked eggs, p. 238.

Broiled Parmesan Zucchini Halves

Preparation time: 10 minutes   Cooking time: 15 minutes
Serves 6

6 medium size zucchini
½ cup water
¾ t. salt
6 t. butter

6 t. Jane's Seasoning Salt
¾ t. coarsley ground black pepper
3 T. grated Parmesan cheese

1. Preheat oven to 350 degrees.
2. Slice zucchini lengthwise and cut off stem end.
3. Place zucchini in ½ cup boiling water with ¾ t. salt. Cover tightly.
4. Cook 5 minutes or until tender crisp.
5. Remove from water and place zucchini halves, skin side down, in oven proof baking dish (pyrex dish, pie pan, etc.).
6. Sprinkle each half with the following: 1 t. butter, 1 t. Jane's Seasoning Salt, ⅛ t. pepper, and ½ T. Parmesan cheese.*
7. Place zucchini in 350 degree oven and bake 10 minutes or until heated through. (Can go in last 10 minutes with crab.)
8. If not brown enough, flip on broiler 1-2 minutes. Sprinkle with paprika and serve.

* Can be done in advance up to this point and refrigerated.

Bloody Mary Aspic Salad

Preparation time: 12 minutes   Serves 8-10

See p. 238 for congealing salads

1 24 oz. bottle Mr. and Mrs. T. or any good Bloody Mary mix
2 T. unflavored gelatin
½ T. Worcestershire sauce
2 T. bottled lemon juice
½ t. bottled onion juice
⅛ t. sugar
Scant ⅛ t. ground cloves
1 3 oz. package cream cheese (optional)

1. Dissolve gelatin in 1 cup Bloody Mary mix.
2. Combine remainder of Bloody Mary mix with Worcester-shire sauce, lemon juice, onion juice, sugar, and cloves in uncovered saucepan. Bring to a boil.
3. Stir gelatin into hot mixture. Mix well, reduce heat, and simmer 5 minutes.
4. Make small balls of cream cheese (about the size of a dime) and place in each mold.
5. Pour hot mixture into individual molds or 1 two quart mold.
6. Refrigerate until firm. Serve with sour cream dressing, sprinkle with paprika, garnish with parsley or olive slice.

Note: This salad freezes well.

Sour Cream Dressing

Preparation time: 5 minutes   Serves 10-12

⅔ cup sour cream   **⅓ cup mayonnaise (no substitutes)**

1. Mix together sour cream and mayonnaise.
2. Refrigerate until ready to use.

Hot Poppy Seed Rolls

Preparation time: 5-10 minutes

1 package Pepperidge Farm Party rolls or bakery equivalent

Poppy Seeds
Butter

1. Preheat oven to 350 degrees.
2. Split rolls in half.
3. Butter each half and sprinkle lightly with poppy seeds.
4. Heat 3-5 minutes until warm and butter has melted or run under broiler until crisp and browned.

French Chocolate Pie

Preparation time: 15 minutes   Serves 6

1 6 oz. Ready-Crust, butter flavored

1 6 oz. package Real chocolate semi sweet chips

4 T. milk

1 8 oz. package cream cheese, softened

1 t. vanilla

2 T. strong coffee (use instant)

2 T. Triple Sec liqueur

1 t. grated orange rind (optional)

1 8 oz. carton whipped topping with real cream

1. Melt chocolate chips in saucepan with 4 T. milk, stirring constantly.
2. Put cream cheese, vanilla, coffee, Triple Sec, and orange rind in blender or mixer.
3. Add melted chocolate and beat until well blended and mixture is smooth.
4. Pour into Ready Crust and refrigerate until set.
5. Spread whipped topping over entire top and garnish with shaved chocolate.
6. Refrigerate until ready to serve.

Note: Can be made several days in advance.

Menu II

Brandied Filet de Boeuf

French Green Beans with Slivered Almonds

Ruby Red Raspberry Salad

Toast Halves of Pepperidge Farm Rolls

Red Wine

Café St. Jacques

with

Whipped Cream and Shaved Chocolate

Brandied Filet de Boeuf

(Fil-lay du Buff)

For years the amateur has shied away from pan-broiling steaks, thinking only the master French chefs could accomplish this treat. Actually, the process is very simple if directions below are followed.

Preparation time: 12 minutes   Cooking time: 10-12 minutes
Serves 4

**4 6 oz. filets (cut 1½-1¾"
thick)**

**¼ t. coarsely ground black
pepper per filet**

1½ T. butter

1½ T. olive oil

**2 4½ oz. cans mushrooms,
drained**

**2 T. minced green onions
or shallots**

2 dashes Tabasco

1 dash Worcestershire

¼ t. bottled lemon juice

1 t. flour

½ cup red burgundy

2 T. brandy

1. Steaks should be at room temperature.
2. Dry each filet thoroughly on paper towels and sprinkle lightly with coarsely ground black pepper, rubbing pepper into filet with palm of hand.
3. Steaks can be cooked immediately or left out covered with wax paper 2 to 3 hours for pepper flavor to penetrate.

4. When ready to cook, place heated platter (or anything that holds heat) beside your cooking skillet.
5. Place 1½ T. butter and 1½ T. olive oil in skillet over moderately high heat until butter foams and almost begins to subside. (This sears the steak without burning.) DO NOT let butter and oil smoke.
6. Sauté steaks on one side 3 to 4 minutes, keeping heat regulated to moderately high. Turn steaks and sauté on other side 3 to 4 minutes. This cooks a medium rare steak.
7. Remove filets to heated platter and reduce heat in skillet to medium low.
8. Add to skillet: drained mushrooms, shallots or onions, Tabasco, Worcestershire, and lemon juice. Cook for 1 minute stirring constantly.
9. Add 1 t. flour stirring until absorbed.
10. Add ½ cup burgundy and 2 T. brandy. Boil rapidly for 2 minutes until sauce is reduced and slightly thickened.
11. Transfer filets to heated serving plates. Spoon sauce over each filet and garnish with parsley.

Note: Rib, T-Bone, or Strip can be substituted for filet. Have the butcher cut steaks 1-1½" thick and trim any excess fat.

French Green Beans with Slivered Almonds

(cook beans before steak)

Preparation time: 10-12 minutes   Serves 4

1 10 oz. package frozen **1 2 oz. package slivered**
 French-style green beans **almonds**
1 T. butter   **salt**
         1 t. butter

1. Cook green beans according to directions. Drain well and set aside.
2. At serving time quickly re-warm green beans and toss with 1 T. melted butter.
3. Sprinkle with slivered almonds.

Note: Can substitute packaged frozen French-style green beans containing Almonds in Butter Sauce.

Toasted Slivered Almonds

Note: These can be done weeks in advance and frozen. Good to have on hand.

1. Spread almonds out on shallow pan.
2. Dot with 1 t. butter and lightly sprinkle with salt.
3. Heat in 300 degree oven until lightly browned, 8-10 minutes.

Ruby Red Raspberry Salad

Preparation time: 13 minutes   Serves 6

1 10 oz. package frozen raspberries, thawed
1 3 oz. package raspberry jello
1 3 oz. package cream cheese
½ cup water

¼ cup orange juice
1 8 oz. can crushed pineapple, undrained
1 2 oz. package English walnuts, chopped
1 t. bottled lemon juice

1. Heat water and orange juice until very hot.
2. Add jello and stir until dissolved.
3. Put hot gelatin mixture and cream cheese in blender and liquefy.
4. Pour into mixing bowl.
5. Add lemon juice, undrained pineapple, raspberries, and walnuts, mixing well.
6. Pour into 6 individual molds or 1 large mold.

Serve with sour cream dressing, p. 87.

Toast Halves Of Twisted Pepperidge Farm Rolls

Preparation time: 8 minutes   Cooking time: 5-6 minutes
Serves 4

**4 Pepperidge Farm
  Twisted Rolls**
butter, ½-1 t. per half roll

**Jane's Seasoning Salt,
  ¼ t. per half roll**
**grated Parmesan cheese,
  ½ t. per half roll**

1. Split rolls lengthwise and lay on cookie sheet.
2. Spread each half liberally with butter.
3. Sprinkle Jane's Seasoning Salt over each half and top
   with grated Parmesan cheese.
4. Place under broiler in center of oven until golden brown.

**Note: Will hold in warm oven without overcooking if
  wrapped in aluminum foil.**

Café St. Jacques

Preparation time: 5-6 minutes   Serves 4

**2 cups strong black hot
  coffee (can use instant)**
4 oz. Kahlua (½ cup)*
2 T. Crème de Cacao

**6-8 heaping T. whipped
  topping with Real cream**
**shaved chocolate
  (optional)**

1. Combine hot coffee, Kahlua, and Crème de Cacao.
2. Pour into heated wine glasses or individual coffee cups.
3. Top with whipped cream topping.
4. Shave or grate a little chocolate over each serving, or
   sprinkle with small amount of cocoa.

* Tia Maria or any coffee flavored liqueur may be substituted.

Menu III

Louisiana Shrimp Curry over Rice

Chilled Pineapple Bits

condiments of:

Chutney. . .Peanuts. . .Raisins

Coconut. . .Bacon. . .Green Onions

Slivered Hard-Cooked Eggs

Hot Bakery French Bread

White Wine

Crème de Menthe over Lime Sherbet

Coffee

Lousiana Shrimp Curry

This sumptuous and especially easy dinner features an intriguing assortment of exotic condiments passed from guest to guest.

Preparation time: 20 minutes   Serves 4

2 lbs. peeled and deveined shrimp
1 chicken boullion cube
1 cup boiling water
5 T. butter
6 T. flour
½ T. dried minced onion

2 cups milk
1¼ t. salt
1½ t. sugar
¼ t. ground ginger
2 t. curry powder
1½ t. bottled lemon juice

1. Dissolve boullion cube in 1 cup boiling water. Set aside.
2. Melt 5 T. butter in saucepan and blend in 6 T. flour.
3. Slowly add 2 cups milk and 1½ T. minced onion, stirring until smooth.
4. Add salt, sugar, ginger, and curry powder. (add ½ t. more for stronger curry flavor)
5. Cook slowly and continue to stir until sauce is smooth and thickened. (the sauce can be made ahead or frozen up to this point)
6. Add 2 lbs. of shrimp and lemon juice to hot mixture.
7. Cook 3 minutes and serve over white rice.

Note: Overcooking ruins shrimp. If shrimp are frozen, drop in hot sauce and cook until they turn pink – about 5 minutes.

Rice

Buy instant or Minute Rice and cook according to directions on box. Allow 1 cup of rice per person for each serving. This can be done in advance and kept warm in pan.

Condiments

(To be assembled in individual bowls and
placed on table ahead of time)

Asterisks * indicate the bare necessities. The greater the variety the more festive!

1 bottle mango chutney (Major Grey's preferred)*

dry roasted peanuts*

package or can of flaked cocoanut*

minced green onions (tops included)

Slivered or chopped hard-cooked eggs (2 sufficient)

Raisins

6-8 slices crumbled bacon

Cold Pineapple Bits

(Takes the place of a salad and is a refreshing
accompaniment to the curry)

2 15 oz. cans chunk pineapple, drained and well chilled

1. Place pineapple in bowl and let guests help themselves.

Hot Bakery French Bread

1 loaf bakery French or   **butter**
Italian bread

1. Preheat oven to 350 degrees.
2. Cut loaf lengthwise from end to end. Do not cut all the way through.
3. Cut crosswise in 1" slices, again not cutting all the way through.
4. Butter each slice well.
5. Heat in 350 degree oven 10–12 minutes or until nicely browned.

Crème de Menthe Over Lime Sherbert

(can be made two or three days ahead)

Preparation time: 10 minutes   Serves 4

2 cups vanilla   **4 T. green Crème de**
  ice cream   **Menthe**
2 cups lime sherbet   **4 green Maraschino**
                    cherries

1. Spoon half vanilla ice cream and half lime sherbet into four individual compotes or ice cream dishes. (Can substitute attractive paper containers.)
2. Dribble 1 T. green Crème de Menthe over each.
3. Cover with foil and freeze.
4. When ready to serve, top each with a green Maraschino cherry.

Menu IV

Oriental Stir-Fried Oyster Beef

Rice

Green Cherry and Pineapple Salad

Orange Sherbet. . .Chinese Fortune Cookies

Oolong or Jasmine Tea

Oriental Stir-Fried Oyster Beef

Stir-frying is an exciting adventure – easy, quick, and economical. Once the meat is sliced and marinating, it is only a matter of minutes until dinner can be served. If you don't own a wok, a large round pan with a curved bottom or an electric skillet will produce the same delicious results.

Preparation time: 30 minutes   Cooking time: 8-10 minutes
Serves 4-6

Marinade

1 lb. flank steak	**1½ t. sugar**
8 T. oyster flavored sauce*	**5 t. cornstarch**
½ t. sesame oil*	**1 t. onion salt**
3 T. soy sauce	**2 T. Worcestershire sauce**

FOR COOKING

peanut oil	**1 garlic clove**

Vegetables

1 14 oz. can bamboo shoots*	**¾ of 1 piece crystallized ginger, minced**
1 14 oz. can bean sprouts*	**4 green onions, minced (include part of tops)**
1 8 oz. can sliced water chestnuts*	
2 6 oz. boxes frozen snow pea pods**	

*Available in Chinese food section of most grocery stores.

**Available in frozen vegetable section of most grocery stores.

1. Slice flank steak paper thin – no thicker than ⅛ inch and no longer than 2 inches. Make all pieces as uniform as possible. Set aside.
2. Place in colander to thaw and drain: snow peas, bamboo shoots, bean sprouts, and water chestnuts.
3. Combine in a mixing bowl the marinade of oyster sauce, sesame oil, soy sauce, sugar, cornstarch, onion salt, and Worcestershire, stirring until well blended.
4. Add sliced pieces of flank steak and toss until thoroughly coated.
5. Set aside at room temperature for at least 30 minutes. (Mixture can be made ahead and refrigerated up to 24 hours.)
6. Rub cooking pan with garlic clove and discard.
7. Heat 2 T. peanut oil at moderately high temperature.
8. Place green onions and tops in pan, stir-frying for 1-1½ minutes. Remove and set aside.
9. Place meat in hot skillet. Cook approximately 2 minutes, stirring constantly. Remove from fire and set aside.
10. Add 1 T. peanut oil to pan.
11. Add snow peas, bamboo shoots, bean sprouts, water chestnuts, and minced ginger. Stir-fry 2 minutes or until crisply cooked.
12. Return meat and green onions to pan, stirring well and heating thoroughly.
13. Arrange on bed of rice (¾-1 cup rice per person), garnish with parsley and serve immediately.
14. Pass a pitcher of Magi Sauce* for additional seasoning.

Rice

Preparation time: 8 minutes

1 box instant Minute Rice   **butter and salt**

1. Follow directions on box of rice for required number of servings.
2. Have water boiling for instant rice while slicing flank steak or making marinade.
3. Cook rice and set aside until ready to serve. (With heated plates and steaming hot oyster beef, rice will keep warm.)

Green Cherry and Pineapple Salad

Preparation time: 6 minutes   Serves 4-6

1 16 oz. can chilled
pineapple slices

1 4 oz. jar green
Maraschino cherries

1. Drain chilled pineapple and blot with paper towels.
2. Divide pineapple slices evenly on salad plates.
3. Top with green cherries.

Note: Lettuce is not necessary in an Oriental dinner. This can be prepared, covered with plastic wrap, and refrigerated several hours in advance.

Orange Sherbert and Fortune Cookies

1 qt. orange sherbet

1 package Chinese
Fortune Cookies

1. Scoop orange sherbet into dessert bowls and freeze in advance.
2. At serving time, remove sherbet, place on plate along with Fortune Cookie.

Note: Fortune Cookies (available in most grocery stores) are a fun conversation piece and the sherbet a needed "light" finale to a good Oriental meal.

Menu V

Chicken Camille

Long Grain and Wild Rice

Artichoke Hearts

Bing Cherry Salad

White Wine

Orange Chiffon Surprise

Coffee

Chicken Camille

A real palate pleaser — decidedly different!

Preparation time: 15 minutes   Cooking time: 30 minutes
Serves 4

4 chicken breasts
2 8 oz. cartons sour cream
4 oz. crumbled Roquefort
  cheese

1 clove garlic, crushed
4 T. butter or margarine
salt and pepper
  (approximately ⅛ t. per
  chicken breast)

1. Sprinkle each chicken breast lightly with salt and pepper.
2. Rub skillet with crushed garlic clove and discard.
3. Melt 4T butter over moderately high heat and place chicken breasts in skillet.
4. Brown on both sides in melted butter and remove to baking dish when browned. About 10-12 minutes.
5. While chicken is browning, preheat oven to 350° degrees
6. Mix sour cream and Roquefort together. Pour over chicken breasts.
7. Cover baking dish and bake 30 minutes. DO NOT OVERCOOK or sour cream will separate.
8. Place chicken breasts on individual plates, spooning ample amount of sauce over each. Sprinkle with paprika and garnish with parsley.
9. Pass remaining sauce at table.

Long Grain and Wild Rice

(make ahead of time)

Preparation time: 5 minutes   Cooking time: 25 minutes
Serves 6

1 box Uncle Ben's Long   **2⅓ cups water**
Grain and Wild Rice   **1 T. butter**
Mixture

1. Put water and butter into saucepan and bring to boil.
2. Stir in contents of box and bring to boil.
3. Cover tightly and reduce to simmer.
4. Cook 23 minutes. (This can be done ahead to this point)
5. Reheat 5 minutes prior to serving.

Artichoke Hearts

Preparation time: 5 minutes   Serves 4

1 18 oz. can artichoke   **1 T. butter, melted**
hearts

1. Heat artichoke hearts in their juice until hot throughout.
2. Drain and pour 1 T. melted butter over artichokes, tossing
   to coat.
3. Divide artichoke hearts equally among four plates and
   serve.

Bing Cherry Salad

(see rule for congealed salad, p. 238)

Preparation time: 10 minutes   Serves 10

**2 16 oz. cans pitted
Bing Cherries
1 6 oz. box black cherry
jello**

**½ cup bourbon
1 cup water**

1. Drain cherries and reserve 2 cups of juice.
2. Heat water and juice until hot.
3. Add jello and stir until dissolved.
4. Add cherries and bourbon and pour into lightly oiled individual or one large mold.
5. Refrigerate until set and ready to serve.
6. Place on bed of Red or Iceberg lettuce and surround with cantaloupe strips if in season.

Top with sour cream dressing, p. 87

Orange Chiffon Surprise

Preparation time: 10 minutes   Serves 6-8

**1 bakery orange chiffon
cake
1 20 oz. can crushed
pineapple, drained
1 2 oz. pkg. slivered
toasted almonds
(optional)**

**1 pkg. vanilla instant
pudding
1 large container whipped
topping with real cream**

1. Slice crosswise orange chiffon cake making 3 layers.
2. Mix pudding, pineapple, and whipped topping together.
3. Spread on each layer and then cover entire cake.
4. Sprinkle with toasted almonds. (see p. 92)
5. Freeze or refrigerate. Will keep in refrigerator several days.

A TOUCH OF ITALY
SHOWSTOPPER QUICK!!!

Spaghetti . . . Fettucine . . . Tetrazinni

A TOUCH OF ITALY
SHOWSTOPPER QUICK!!!

Campari Aperitif
Antipasto Italiante
Pasta Napoli (Spaghetti)
Parmesan Cheese
Hot Garlic Bread
Fresh Fruit and Cheese Tray

Fettucine
Angelo Salad
with
Italian Mustard Dressing
Bread Sticks
Sicilian Chocolate Torte

Chicken Tetrazinni
Herbed Cherry Tomatoes
Braised Peas Romano
Bread Sticks
Three Fruit Granita

Menu I

Campari Aperitif

Antipasto Italiante

Pasta Napoli (Spaghetti)

Parmesan Cheese

Hot Garlic Bread

Red Wine

Fresh Fruit and Cheese Tray

Coffee

Campari Aperitif

Preparation time: 10 minutes   Serves 4

¾ cup Italian Sweet Vermouth
¾ cup Campari
¾ cup dry white wine

crushed ice
1 small bottle dry soda water
4 thin slices lemon

1. Put Vermouth, Campari, and wine into cocktail shaker or plastic juice container.
2. Add enough crushed ice (or ice cubes) to chill well.
3. Shake vigorously.
4. Strain into chilled wine glasses, leaving enough room for soda water.
5. Add a dash of soda water to each glass and garnish with lemon slice.

Antipasto Italianate

Preparation time

Preparation time: 10-30 minutes
(time based on number of selections)
Serves 4-8

(Choose all of following zesty hors d'oeuvres or minimum of six)

1 small bottle marinated artichoke hearts
1 small bottle marinated mushrooms
1 small can ripe olives
1 small bottle green olives
1 can anchovies, drained
1 bunch curly endive
Cherry tomatoes marinated

1 can sardines, drained
1 16 oz. jar Mild Giardiniera Mixed Vegetables
4 hard-cooked eggs, peeled and quartered
Thin slices of Prosciutto (ham)* wrapped around melon slices
Thin slices salami* rolled up
Toothpicks

1. Wash and drain endive. Refrigerate wrapped in paper towel and air tight plastic bag until ready for use.
2. Arrange endive on a platter, interspersing hors d'oeuvres decoratively.
3. Present as a first course and let guests help themselves.

* Buy 3 oz. package of thin sliced ham or salami, roll up and secure with toothpicks.

(Example of color balanced variety: marinated mushroom, Mild Giardiniera Mixed Vegetables, ripe olives, hard-cooked eggs, quartered, thin slices of rolled up salami.)

Pasta Napoli

(Spaghetti with Meat Sauce)

MEAT SAUCE

Preparation time: 18 minutes   Cooking time: 30 minutes
Serves 4 generously

1 T. olive oil
1 lb. lean ground beef
½ T. instant minced dried onion
2 packages Spaghetti Sauce mix (Williams preferred)*
1¼ t. Italian Herb Seasoning
1½ cups water (add additional ½ cup water if cooking longer than 30 minutes)

¼ t. sugar (optional)
1 15 oz. can tomato sauce
1 8 oz. can tomatoes, undrained
1 4 oz. jar mushrooms, drained
1 garlic clove, crushed
¼ cup dry red wine or burgundy

1. Brown meat in 1 T. olive oil.
2. Drain well and return to pan.
3. Add to meat: onion, Spaghetti Sauce mix, Italian seasoning, water, sugar (optional), tomato sauce, tomatoes and juice, mushrooms, and crushed garlic clove.
4. Stir to mix well.
5. Cover and bring to rolling boil.
6. Reduce heat to simmer and cook 20 minutes, stirring occasionally.
7. Add ¼ cup Burgundy and bring to boil.
8. Reduce heat and simmer 8-10 minutes, stirring occasionally.

* Be sure that the Spaghetti Sauce mix purchased calls for ½ lb. ground meat. If mix specifies 1 lb. ground beef, use only 1 package instead of 2 packages called for in above recipe.

Spaghetti

Preparation and cooking time: 15 minutes   Serves 4

**1 lb. spaghetti (1 16 oz.
  package)
1 T. oil**

**2 T. salt
12 cups boiling water**

1. In large saucepan bring water, oil, and salt to a boil.
2. Add spaghetti.
3. Do not cover, but adjust heat to keep water boiling during entire cooking process.
4. Cook approximately 15 minutes or until tastes tender— should have a slight bite but not mushy.
5. Drain and divide equally among four heated plates.
6. Spoon meat sauce over each helping. Garnish with parsley.
7. Pass Parmesan cheese (freshly grated if possible) at the table.

Hot Garlic Bread

Preparation time: 12 minutes   Serves 8

**1 loaf French bread
  (12″ long)**
1-2 garlic cloves, mashed
¼ t. paprika

1 stick butter
¼ t. salt
**1 T. minced parsley
  (optional)**

1. Melt butter in small saucepan.
2. Add garlic cloves, paprika, and salt.
3. Simmer over low heat 8-10 minutes, stirring occasionally and watching to see that butter does not burn.
4. While garlic butter is cooking, slice bread lengthwise not cutting all the way through to bottom crust.
5. Make 8 slices crosswise, again not cutting through to bottom crust.
6. Paint both sides of each piece liberally with garlic butter.
7. Use remaining butter to paint top and sides of loaf.
8. Sprinkle minced parsley over top of loaf.
9. Cook 350 degrees for 15 minutes or until bread is hot, crusty, and golden brown.

* Buy garlic bread already prepared if bakery or deli stocks it.

Note: Freezes well, but do not cook until ready to use.

Fresh Fruit and Cheese Tray

(doubles as an inviting centerpiece and dessert)

Preparation time: 10 minutes   Serves 4

2 ripe pears
1 tart apple
½ lb. seedless green
grapes
½ lb. purple grapes

4-6 oz. Brie (bree)*
4-6 oz. Bell Paese
(bel-pah-ay'-ze)*
4-6 oz. Aged Cheddar*
Melba toast and thin crisp
crackers

1. Arrange cheese, pears, and apples on a tray or platter that will serve as a centerpiece in middle of table.
2. Cut grapes into small clusters and scatter decoratively among fruit and cheese.
3. Furnish knives to cut fruit and additional spreaders for cheese.
4. Enhance fruit and cheese tray with fresh mint and evergreen.
5. Put melba toast and crackers in baskets on each side of tray.

* Choose a soft, semi-soft, and semi-firm to firm cheese for variety. Ask local cheese shop to help with selections.

Note: Always serve cheese at room temperature for full flavor.

Menu II

Fettucine

Angelo Salad

with

Italian Mustard Dressing

Bread Sticks

White Wine

Sicilian Chocolate Torte

Coffee

Fettucine

Preparation and cooking time: 15 minutes   Serves 4

1 8 oz. package fettucine noodles

8-10 cups water

¾ t. salt

8 T. (1 stick) butter softened (no substitutes)

1 cup whipping cream

¾ cup freshly grated Parmesan cheese

¾ t. (or more) freshly ground black pepper

Top only of 1 green onion, finely minced (optional)

Heaping bowl of freshly grated Parmesan cheese for table

1. Heat oven to 300 degrees.
2. Place serving bowl or casserole dish in oven to warm.
3. Bring water and salt to a boil.
4. Drop in fettucine and stir gently for a minute until strands are separated. Cook 7-8 minutes after water has resumed a second boil.
5. While noodles are cooking, combine softened butter, cream, and cheese.
6. Beat by hand or with an electric mixer until ingredients are well mixed, light, and fluffy.
7. Drain fettucine into a colander. Shake colander vigorously to be sure noodles are well drained. Transfer to hot serving bowl.
8. Pour butter cream mixture, black pepper, and optional green minced onion over fettucine.
9. Toss well until each strand is coated.
10. Taste, correct seasonings, and serve.
11. Pass bowl of Parmesan cheese at table.

Angelo Salad

Preparation time: 15 minutes   Serves 4-6

1 head crisp Romaine lettuce
1-2 oz. can anchovies
½ cup Feta cheese (available in delis and grocery dairy departments)

1 jar mild golden green peppers, (Towie Early California 15½ oz. jar of sufficient mildness and flavor)
Italian Mustard Dressing (recipe follows)

1. To prepare Romaine, separate choice leaves, discarding others, and wash thoroughly. Dry by letting drip in colander and then wrapping lightly in an absorbent tea towel or soft paper toweling until water evaporated. Seal in plastic wrap and place in vegetable drawer of refrigerator until ready for use.
2. Measure and place in plastic covered bowls and refrigerate:
   6 green peppers cut into 6-8 pieces each; anchovies cut coarsely into tiny bits; crumble cheese.
3. Make Italian Mustard Dressing (see following recipe) and refrigerate.
4. While fettucine is cooking, tear Romaine into approximately 3 inch pieces and place in salad bowl.
5. Measure 1 T. Italian Mustard Dressing and toss repeatedly over Romaine by lifting leaves gently with a large fork and spoon until each leaf has a light coating. Return to refrigerator along with number of individual salad bowls needed.*
6. Before serving fettucine: Remove salad bowls and salad ingredients from refrigerator; add mild green peppers, Feta cheese, and anchovies to Romaine in salad bowl; toss gently with 2 T. of Italian dressing.**

continued on next page

7. Serve plentiful helpings into each individual chilled bowl and place on table.

* Salad can be left in larger bowl and served at table if preferred.

** Caution on amount of salad dressing; too much spoils crispness and flavor.

Italian Mustard Dressing

Preparation time: 5 minutes   Serves 4-6 — makes 1 cup

½ **cup olive oil**
1 **garlic clove, split**
2 **T. wine vinegar**
1 **T. Dijon mustard**

¼ **t. salt**
½ **t. coarsely ground black pepper**
½ **t. oregano**

1. Pour ½ cup olive oil in a bowl. Add split garlic clove.
2. Add 2 T. wine vinegar, beating with wire whisk.
3. Add mustard, salt, pepper and oregano, continuing to beat until well mixed.
4. After 5 minutes remove garlic cloves and refrigerate dressing in jar.

Bread Sticks

Serves 4

1 6 oz. package bread sticks (sesame preferred)

1 stick butter

1. Place bread sticks in a basket on table and serve with butter.

Sicilian Chocolate Torte

(intriguingly different)

Preparation time: 15-18 minutes   Serves 18-20

(keeps in refrigerator for a week or can be made ahead and frozen)

1 16 oz. Sara Lee All Butter Pound Cake
1 15 oz. carton Ricotta cheese

¼ cup powdered sugar
4 T. orange flavored liqueur

1. Slice cake horizontally into 4 even slabs.
2. Combine Ricotta cheese, powdered sugar, and liqueur and beat by hand until well mixed. (1-2 minutes)
3. Place bottom slice of cake on flat surface and spread with ⅓ of Ricotta mixture. Repeat layers until all cake slices are used up. End with a cake slice on top.
4. Press loaf firmly together and be sure all sides are even.
5. If weather is warm, refrigerate until filling is set before icing.

continued on next page

Frosting

**1 16 oz. can Creamy
Deluxe ready to spread
chocolate frosting**
1 T. water

1 T. instant coffee
1 t. vanilla
**1 2 oz. pkg. toasted
slivered almonds
(optional)**

1. Dissolve coffee in water.
2. In a small mixing bowl, combine coffee, vanilla, and frosting.
3. Beat until mixture is smooth and ingredients well combined — about 1 minute.
4. Frost tops and sides of torte, swirling chocolate decoratively.
5. Sprinkle with toasted almonds. Press any loose almonds gently into frosting.
6. Cover and refrigerate.
7. Better taste if made 24 hours in advance.

Menu III

Chicken Tetrazinni

Braised Peas Romano

Herbed Cherry Tomatoes

Bread Sticks

Red Wine

Three Fruit Granita

Coffee

TO COOK CHICKEN FOR TETRAZZINI*
(or buy pre-cooked chicken at deli or grocery)

6 chicken breasts   **½ onion quartered**

2 celery stalks   **½ t. salt**

1. Cover chicken breasts, celery, and onion with water.
2. Add salt and bring to boil.
3. Cover tightly and let simmer on low heat until tender and meat falls off bone when pricked with a fork (approximately 30 minutes).
4. Let chicken cool in its own liquid.
5. Save liquid for soup or to cook spaghetti in following recipe.

* Turkey may be substituted.

Chicken Tetrazinni

(make ahead supper buffet)

Preparation time: 25 minutes   Cooking time: 30 minutes
Serves 8

6 cups water
½ t. salt
1 T. olive or cooking oil
1 8 oz. package spaghetti broken into pieces
2-2½ cups cooked diced chicken or turkey
1 4 oz. can mushrooms, undrained
1 T. minced dried onions
¼ t. Tabasco
¼ t. marjoram

1 10¾ oz. can Cream of Chicken soup
1 13 oz. can evaporated milk
1 4 oz. package grated sharp Cheddar cheese
½ cup grated Parmesan cheese
2 T. chopped pimento (optional)
2 T. dry sherry (optional)

1. Put 6 cups water on to boil, adding salt and oil.
2. Drop spaghetti into boiling water and cook 18 minutes.
3. Drain mushrooms and reserve liquid.
4. While spaghetti is cooking, put into large mixing bowl: mushroom liquid, minced onion, celery salt, Tabasco, marjoram, Cream of Chicken soup, and evaporated milk.
5. Mix until ingredients are well blended.
6. Add mushrooms, chicken, and pimento, mixing well.
7. Drain spaghetti and rinse under cold water. (This eliminates starch.)
8. Divide spaghetti into 3 equal parts.
9. Cover bottom of a 9 x 13 inch pyrex dish with layers of: a third of spaghetti, half the chicken mixture, and half the sharp cheese; repeat, ending up with layer of spaghetti.
10. Sprinkle ½ cup Parmesan cheese over top.
11. Bake 30 minutes at 400 degrees or until hot and bubbly. Let set 10 minutes before serving.

Note: Can be made in advance and frozen.

Braised Peas Romano

Preparation time: 10 minutes   Serves 4 (double if serving 8)

1 10 oz. package frozen peas
⅓ cup finely chopped red onion
2 T. butter

1 chicken bouillon cube dissolved in ½ cup hot water (or ½ cup chicken stock)
¼ t. Italian Herb Seasoning
¼ t. black pepper

1. Melt 2 T. butter in a 1-2 qt. saucepan.
2. Add finely chopped onions and cook until soft, but not mushy (4-5 minutes).
3. Stir in chicken stock, Italian Herb Seasoning, and black pepper.
4. Add frozen peas, cover, bring to a boil.
5. Reduce heat to medium and cook 3 minutes.
6. Remove from heat and let stand 5 minutes.
7. Serve peas in a heated bowl.

Herbed Cherry Tomatoes

(Prepare 2-4 hours ahead)

Preparation time: 7 minutes   Serves 8

2 pints cherry tomatoes
1 cup olive oil
¼ t. salt

¼ t. oregano
2 garlic cloves pressed

1. Wash and stem cherry tomatoes. Pat dry.
2. Combine olive oil, seasoning, and pressed garlic in bowl. Stir to mix well.
3. Add cherry tomatoes, tossing to coat well.
4. Let marinate 2-4 hours.
5. Serve cold or at room temperature.

Bread Sticks
(see p. 118)

Three Fruit Granita

Preparation time: 6 minutes   Makes 8 one half cup servings

1 medium ripe banana
1 15½ oz. can crushed
pineapple, undrained

2 cups whipped topping
with real cream
1 6 oz. can frozen
lemonade concentrate,
thawed

1. Combine all ingredients in blender, mixing on high until well blended.
2. Spoon into container, individual glasses, or paper cups.
3. Place in freezer until firm.
4. At serving time top with a green or red maraschino cherry.

AFTER THE GAME

Hot and Robust
Simmering on the Stove Ready to Serve

AFTER THE GAME

South of the Border Chili
Shredded Sharp Cheese and Minced Onions
Make Ahead Easy Superchef Slaw
Golden Rum Cake

Low Country Fish Chowder
Daiquiri Lime Fruit Salad
Corn Muffins
Fantastically Easy Mocha Pie

Zippy Sausage Rice Casserole
Tomato Vegetable Medley
Hot French Bread
Strawberries with Cream of Liqueur Almond

French Onion Soup
Hunks of Crusty Hot Bread
Colorful Fruit Basket
10 Minute Luscious Lemon Pie

Menu I

South of the Border Chili

Shredded Sharp Cheese and Minced Onions

Crackers or Corn Chips

Make Ahead Easy Superchef Slaw

Iced Mugs of Cold Beer

Golden Rum Cake

Coffee

South of the Border Chili

Preparation time: 10 minutes   Cooking time: 15 minutes
Serves 4 heartily

1 lb. lean ground beef
1 16 oz. can tomato sauce
1 15 oz. can chili beans,
  Mexican style
1 15 oz. can kidney or
  pinto beans
2 T. instant dried minced
  onion

1 pkg. chili seasoning
  (Williams preferred)
⅓ cup water*
½ t. salt (optional)
1 clove garlic pressed

1. In medium size sauce pan, brown beef and drain well.
2. Return drained beef to pan and add: tomato sauce, beans (juice and all), onion, chili seasoning, water, salt, and pressed garlic clove.
3. Stir to blend well.
4. Bring to a boil, reduce heat, and simmer 15 minutes, stirring occasionally.
5. Serve piping hot with following condiments.

continued on next page

Note: Use 1 pkg. chili seasoning that calls for 2 lbs. ground beef, or if pkg. specifies 1 lb. beef, use 2 packages. This freezes well.

*Add ⅓ cup water if re-heating or chili becomes too thick.

Condiments for Chili

1 medium onion
Saltines or corn chips

1 cup grated sharp Cheddar cheese

1. Mince finely 1 medium onion. Place in small serving bowl.
2. Place 1 cup grated sharp Cheddar cheese in another small serving bowl.
3. Put saltines or corn chips in wooden or wicker basket beside bowls of cheese and onion.
4. Let guest help themselves to chili and condiments.

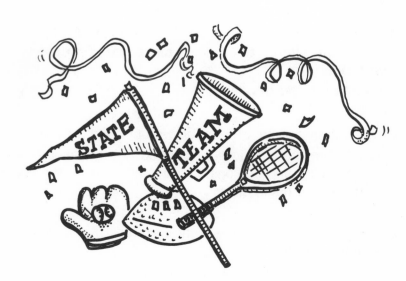

Make-Ahead Easy Superchef Slaw

Preparation time: 25 minutes
Serves 8–10

Slaw

1 medium zucchini,
  chopped
1 cup chopped celery
2 medium onions,
  chopped

1 green pepper, chopped
1 large head cabbage,
  shredded
⅞ cup of sugar

Dressing

¾ cup salad oil
1 cup cider vinegar
2 t. sugar

1 T. salt
1 t. dry mustard
1 t. celery seed

1. Mix together zucchini, celery, onions, green pepper, and cabbage.
2. Sprinkle ⅞ cup sugar over top and set aside.
3. Combine all dressing ingredients in saucepan and bring to boil. Reduce heat and simmer 5 minutes. Let cool to room temperature.
4. Pour over slaw mixture, cover tightly, and refrigerate for 3 days prior to serving.

*Make slaw 3 days in advance for best flavor. Keeps several weeks in refrigerator.

Golden Rum Cake

SEE DESSERT CHAPTER, P. 213

Menu II

Low Country Fish Chowder

Daiquiri Lime Fruit Salad

Corn Muffins

White Wine

Fantastically Easy Mocha Pie

Coffee

Low Country Fish Chowder

(make day before — add fish and clams at last min.)

Preparation time: 30 minutes
Serves 4

**1 16 oz. package skinless
flounder filets***
1 6 oz. can clams
1 cup chopped celery
1 cup chopped onion
**2 cups diced raw potatoes
(2 small to medium
potatoes)**
**1 13 oz. can evaporated
milk**

⅛-¼ t. garlic powder
¾ t. curry powder
½ t. salt
½ t. pepper
½ t. paprika
¼ t. lemon pepper
**1½ cups water for
vegetables**

1. Bring to a boil 1½ cups water in a 4-6 qt. pan, adding celery, onion, and potatoes.
2. Cook until tender, but not mushy. (10-15 minutes)
3. Add evaporated milk, garlic powder, curry powder, salt, pepper, paprika, and lemon pepper to vegetables and liquid, stirring well to combine seasoning with vegetables.
4. Cut up flounder into bite sized pieces.
5. Add flounder and undrained clams.

continued on next page

6. Bring chowder to a rolling boil and cook five minutes.
7. Serve immediately.

*Any MILD white fish like crappie, sole, or whiting can be substituted.

Daiquiri Lime Fruit Salad

(see rule for congealing salads, p. 238)

Preparation time: 10 minutes
Serves 8–10

1 30 oz. can fruit cocktail
1 15½ oz. can crushed pineapple
1 cup hot water

1 6 oz. package lime jello
2 9/16 oz. envelopes Holland House Instant Daiquiri Cocktail Mix (non-alcoholic)

1. Drain juice from fruit cocktail and pineapple. (totals 2 cups liquid)
2. Heat juice and water until hot.
3. Dissolve jello in hot liquid.
4. Add Daiquiri mix, pineapple, and fruit cocktail. Mix well.
5. Pour into lightly oiled 9 × 13 inch pyrex dish or 10 individual molds.
6. Refrigerate until ready to serve.
7. At serving time add a dollop of mayonnaise or Sour Cream Dressing (p. 87) and sprinkle lightly with paprika.

Corn Muffins

Buy a box of corn muffin mix and follow package directions.

Fantastically Easy Mocha Pie

SEE DESSERT CHAPTER, P. 213

Menu III

Zippy Sausage Rice Casserole

Tomato Vegetable Medley

Hot French Bread

Red Wine

Strawberries with Creme of Liqueur Almond

Coffee

Zippy Sausage Rice Casserole

Preparation time: 15 minutes   Cooking time: 1½ hours
Serves 8

1 lb. hot sausage
1 cup raw rice (not instant)
1 cup chopped onion
1 cup chopped celery
1 cup chopped green pepper
1 10¾ oz. can Cream of Chicken soup

1 10¾ oz. can Cream of Mushroom soup
1 4 oz. can mushrooms, drained
⅔ t. curry powder
½ t. salt
1 t. coarsely ground black pepper
2 cups water

1. Cook sausage until brown.
2. While sausage is cooking, combine Cream of Chicken soup, Cream of Mushroom soup, chopped onions, celery, green pepper, mushrooms, curry powder, salt, and black pepper.
3. Drain sausage well.
4. Add sausage, mushrooms, and rice to chicken and mushroom soup mixture. Stir until well mixed. (can be done in advance to this point and refrigerated overnight)
5. When ready to cook, add 2 cups cold water, mixing well.
6. Cook 325 degrees for 1½ hours or until all liquid is absorbed.

Tomato Vegetable Medley

(see rule for congealing salads, p. 238)
Preparation time: 15 minutes
Serves 12

1 6 oz. (or 2 3 oz.) packages lemon jello
1⅓ cups water
1 16 oz. can whole tomatoes
1 16 oz. can asparagus pieces, drained
1 cup celery, chopped

1 medium cucumber, peeled and chopped
¾ cup mayonnaise (no substitutes)
⅓ cup sour cream
2 T. horseradish
¼ t. Tabasco

1. Put 1⅓ cups water on stove to boil.
2. Drain tomatoes well, reserving juice. (approximately ⅔ cup juice) Set aside.
3. Dissolve jello in boiling water. Stir in reserved tomato juice and remove from heat.
4. Chop tomatoes coarsely and pat with paper towels to remove any excess juice.
5. Combine mayonnaise, sour cream, horseradish, and Tabasco with tomato-jello mixture. Whisk or stir until well mixed.
6. Fold in chopped tomatoes, chopped cucumbers, chopped celery, and asparagus pieces.
7. Pour into a lightly oiled 9 × 13 inch pyrex dish, 12 individual molds, or a two quart ring mold.
8. Serve with sour cream, mayonnaise, and horseradish dressing.

Dressing

⅓ cup mayonnaise (no substitutes)
⅓ cup sour cream

1 t. horseradish

1. Combine all ingredients and stir until well blended.
2. Refrigerate until ready to use.

Hot French Bread

1 loaf bakery French   **butter**
 or Italian bread

1. Preheat oven to 350 degrees.
2. Cut loaf lengthwise from end to end. Do not cut all the way through.
3. Cut crosswise in 1" slices, again not cutting all the way through.
4. Butter each slice well.
5. Heat in 350° oven 10-12 minutes or until nicely browned.

Strawberries with Crème of Liqueur Almond
SEE DESSERT CHAPTER, P. 213

Menu IV

French Onion Soup

Hunks of Crusty Hot Bread

Colorful Fruit Basket

10 Minute Luscious Lemon Pie

French Onion Soup

Preparation time: 15-18 minutes   Serves 2 heartily, 3 well

1 14½ oz. can Swanson's pure beef broth
2 cups water
1 package Lipton or Knorr Onion Soup Mix and Dip Mix
3 T. instant minced onions

½ T. dry Vermouth
1 Pepperidge Farm French roll or equivalent
Monterey Jack cheese
Parmesan cheese

1. Preheat oven to 350 degrees.
2. Combine beef broth, water, onion soup mix, and minced onion in pan and bring to boil.
3. Reduce heat to simmer.
4. Cut French roll into cubes and pop in oven for 12 minutes.
5. Let soup simmer 10 minutes.
6. Add Vermouth and pour into warm oven proof bowls.
7. Divide cubed French bread evenly among bowls and top with thin slices of Monterey Jack cheese — 3 to 4 slices per bowl.
8. Sprinkle Parmesan cheese lightly over top.
9. Pop under broiler until cheese begins to melt.

Note: If not serving immediately, place soup in warm 200 degree oven and garnish with bread and cheese at last minute.

Hunks of Crusty Hot Bread
Preparation time: 10 minutes   Serves 4

1 package Pepperidge   **Butter**
Farm French rolls

1. Split each roll in half, but do not cut all the way through.
2. Liberally butter each half.
3. Wrap aluminum foil and place in 350 degree oven to heat when ready to serve.
4. Cook approximately 15 minutes or until lightly browned and crusty.

Colorful Fruit Basket
In a large basket on counter place a tempting assortment of fresh fruit with ample number of knives for cutting.

Tart apples   **Bananas**
Ripe pears   **Green and Red Grapes**
Tangerines

10-Minute Luscious Lemon Pie
SEE DESSERT CHAPTER, P. 213.

IN T-SHIRTS AND BLUE JEANS...
LET'S HAVE A PICNIC

Patio • Poolside • Backyard

IN T-SHIRTS AND BLUE JEANS...
LET'S HAVE A PICNIC

Fiesta Enchiladas
Monterey Rice
Mexican Corn Bread
Pina Colada Torte

Kielbasa and Caraway Kraut
Black Buns and Hot Mustard
German Potato Salad
Tomatoes and Cucumbers Vinaigrette
Chocolate Mint Ice Cream Bars

Barbecued Brisket
Au Gratin Potatoes
Celebration Slaw
Hot French Bread
Ice Cold Watermelon

Bucket Fried Chicken
Beans and Chili
Escalloped Pineapple
Crusty Cheese Loaf
Mile High Strawberry Pie

Menu I
Mexican Fiesta—Picnic Style

Bright colors…lots of candles…music!
Gaily colored paper cloths, napkins, and plates…mix and match!

Fiesta Enchiladas
with
Sour Cream, Tomatoes, and Avocados
Monterey Rice
Mexican Corn Bread
Pina Colada Torte
Sangria…Cold Beer
Mexican Coffee

Fiesta Enchiladas

Preparation time: 20 minutes   Cooking time: 15 minutes
Makes 12

12 corn tortillas
1½ lbs. lean ground beef
1 16 oz. can tomato sauce
2 packages enchilada seasoning mix
2½ cups water
1 pinch sugar
1 T. dried minced onion
⅛ t. garlic powder

2 cups sharp Cheddar cheese (2 4 oz. pkgs.)
1 8 oz. carton sour cream
3 ripe tomatoes, minced and drained
3 ripe avocados, cut into slivers
toothpicks

1. Brown beef in skillet and drain well.
2. While beef is browning, combine tomato sauce, seasoning mix, water, sugar, onion, and garlic powder in saucepan.
3. Bring to a boil, reduce heat, and simmer 8-10 minutes.
4. Soften corn tortillas. Put in steamer or in colander over simmering water until soft enough to roll — only takes a minute or two. Do not let water touch tortillas.
5. Combine browned and drained ground beef, ¾ cup of grated cheese, and 2 cups sauce in mixing bowl. Stir until well mixed.
6. Spoon meat mixture into tortillas; roll up and secure with a toothpick or place seam side down in baking dish.
7. Pour rest of sauce evenly over rolled tortillas. Sprinkle with remaining cheese.
8. Bake 350 degrees 15 minutes.
9. Remove from oven and spread 1 cup sour cream (room temperature) over enchiladas. Sprinkle avocado slices and minced tomatoes over entire top. Serve.

Note: Enchiladas can be made ahead and refrigerated or frozen. Let come to room temperature before baking. To prepare avocados and minced tomatoes in advance — sprinkle avocados with lemon juice and cover tightly; salt and pepper minced tomatoes and wrap in paper towel. Refrigerate until ready to use.

Monterey Rice

Preparation time: 12 minutes   Cooking time: 30 minutes
Serves 8

2¼ cups instant Minute rice
2 cups water
¾ t. salt
1 T. butter

1½ cups sour cream
1 4 oz. can chopped mild green chilies, drained
1 6 oz. package sliced Monterey Jack cheese

1. Preheat oven to 350 degrees.
2. Put water on to boil.
3. Add rice, salt, and butter when water has reached boiling point.
4. Stir and remove from stove. Let set 5-6 minutes or until all water is absorbed and rice is tender and fluffy.
5. While rice is cooking, tear cheese into bite size pieces.
6. On bottom of a buttered casserole (8 x 8) place ¹/₃ of the rice. Smooth ¹/₃ of the sour cream on top of rice. Sprinkle ¹/₃ of chili peppers on top of sour cream and top with ¹/₃ of cheese.
7. Repeat layers twice, ending up with cheese on top.
8. Bake 30 minutes at 350 degrees. Sprinkle with paprika and garnish with parsley.

Mexican Corn Bread

SEE P. 196 FOR RECIPE

Pina Colada Torte

SEE P. 219 FOR RECIPE

Sangria

Preparation time: 10 minutes   Serves 8 (1 glass each)

2 cups Burgundy or any dry red wine

3 cups water

1 6 oz. can frozen limeade, undiluted and thawed

Slices of an orange, a lemon, and a lime (or use only one fruit)

1. Combine Burgundy, water, and thawed limeade in glass pitcher or punch bowl.
2. Slice fruit.
3. Put half of the sliced fruit into pitcher, mix well, refrigerating until cold.
4. At serving time, garnish each glass with a piece of sliced fruit and a maraschino cherry held on a toothpick.

Mexican Coffee

Preparation time: 5 minutes   Serves 4

4 cups water

4 T. instant coffee

½ cup dark brown sugar

⅛ t. ground cinnamon

4 whole cloves

1. Combine water, coffee, sugar, cinnamon and cloves in saucepan.
2. Bring to a boil, stirring until sugar is dissolved.
3. Reduce heat and simmer 10 minutes. Serve hot.

Note: Can be made a day in advance and reheated. Freezes well.

Menu II
Bavarian Oktoberfest

A wheelbarrow full of iced beer…the music of an
umph pah pah band!

Kielbasa and Caraway Kraut
Black Buns and Hot Mustard
German Potato Salad
Tomatoes and Cucumbers Vinaigrette
Chocolate Mint Ice Cream Bars
Cold Beer…Coffee

Kielbasa and Caraway Kraut

(cook and serve in same dish)

Preparation time: 12 minutes
Cooking time: 45 minutes plus 20 minutes   Serves 8

**2 lbs. Polska Kielbasa or
any fully cooked German
or Polish sausage**

**2 32 oz. cans sauerkraut,
drained and rinsed under
cold water**

½ cup dry white wine

1½ t. caraway seeds
½ t. black pepper
2 T. light brown sugar
**1 tart apple, peeled and
halved**
10 whole cloves

1. Preheat oven to 350 degrees.
2. Place drained sauerkraut in 1½ qt. oven proof baking dish.
3. Add wine, caraway seeds, black pepper, and brown sugar. Toss to mix well.
4. Stick 5 whole cloves in each half of peeled apple and bury in sauerkraut.
5. Cover tightly and bake in 350 degree oven for 45 minutes.
6. While sauerkraut is cooking, split sausage in half and then cut into pieces that fit inside black buns.
7. Sauté in skillet until lightly browned and grease is extracted, approximately 10 minutes. Drain well.
8. At end of 45 minutes cooking time for sauerkraut, reduce heat to 325 degrees and place sausage over top of Kraut.
9. Cover tightly, return to oven and cook 20 minutes.
10. Before serving, discard apple and drain any liquid from sauerkraut.

**Note: Will hold successfully in a warm oven for an hour
or so.**

Black Buns and Hot Mustard

Serves 8

8-12 black buns bought from deli (or adequate number for guests)
butter

1 jar hot and spicy German mustard

1. Lightly butter insides of each bun.
2. Wrap tightly in foil and heat 10 minutes just before serving.
3. Place mustard in jar on table.
4. Each guest prepares own sandwich with mustard and a liberal amount of kielbasa and kraut spooned into each bun.

German Potato Salad

Preparation time: 6 minutes   Serves 8

1 51 oz. can KRAFT German Style Potato Salad

6 slices bacon

1. Preheat oven to 350 degrees.
2. Place potato salad in oven proof serving dish and heat, covered, 20 minutes or until warm.
3. Fry bacon until crisp. Drain on paper towels.
4. Crumble bacon over top of potato salad and serve.

Tomatoes and Cucumbers Vinaigrette

Preparation time: 12 minutes   Serves 8

3 tomatoes
2 t. cider vinegar
½ t. salt

2 cucumbers (or enough
to make 2 cups, sliced)
¼ t. sugar

1. Peel and slice tomatoes and put on paper towel to drain, refrigerating until ready to serve.
2. Peel cucumbers and slice into thin rounds.
3. Place in salad bowl and toss with:
   4 t. cider vinegar   ¼ t. pepper
   ½ t. salt   ½ t. sugar
4. Let marinate for 15 minutes and refrigerate until ready to serve.
5. Heap cucumbers in center of serving plate, surround with sliced tomatoes and place on picnic table.

Chocolate Mint Ice Cream Bars

Purchased in any grocery frozen food section.

Menu III
Do It Ahead Backyard Barbecue

Barbecued Brisket

Au Gratin Potatoes

Celebration Slaw

Hot French Bread

Ice Cold Watermelon

Beer. . .Iced Tea. . .Coffee

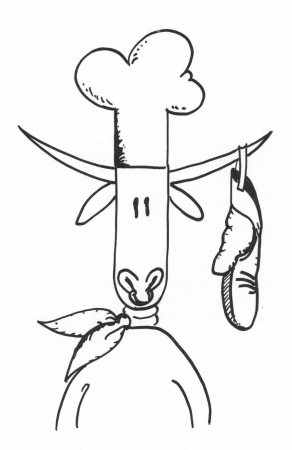

Barbecued Brisket

A surprisingly simple to make picnic favorite. Prepare a day or two in advance, or a couple of weeks and freeze.

Preparation time: 15 minutes
Cooking time: 5-6 hours (just leave in oven on its own—
no basting or looking)
Serves 8-10

1 4½-5 lb. brisket of beef as lean as possible

1 t. salt

3 t. coarsely ground black pepper

2 t. celery seed

2 T. dried parsley

2 T. dried minced onion

1½ t. paprika

40 whole cloves

¼ cup plus 2 T. liquid smoke

1 18 oz. bottle barbecue sauce

1. Spread a piece of heavy duty aluminum foil on counter. Foil should be large enough to cover brisket completely.
2. Place brisket on foil and rub all spices into both sides of brisket. (Divide salt, pepper, celery seed, parsley, onion, paprika, and cloves as evenly as possible between both sides.)
3. Pour liquid smoke over both sides.
4. Wrap tightly in foil and refrigerate overnight—or up to 2 days.
5. Preheat oven to 275 degrees.
6. Place brisket (in foil) in shallow baking pan and bake 275 degrees for 4½-5 hours.
7. Uncover and pour off most of juices—leave about a tablespoon for flavor.
8. Pour ¾ bottle of barbecue sauce over brisket. Turn brisket over so that both sides are coated.
9. Return to oven and bake uncovered for 1 hour.
10. Remove brisket from oven, let stand 15-20 minutes for easy carving.
11. Slice VERY THIN across the grain.

continued on next page

Brisket Sauce

1. When brisket is removed from oven, pour off all sauce into small pan.
2. Add remaining barbecue sauce.
3. Thin with a little water if too thick.
4. Heat just before serving.

Note: Brisket can be sliced well ahead or day or two before if slices are wrapped in aluminum foil and a little sauce dribbled to keep moist. Reheat in warm oven.

Brisket is also excellent for hot barbecued sandwiches. Put thin slices of brisket in German black bread buns, spooning a little warm sauce in each.

Au Gratin Potatoes

Preparation time: 7 minutes   Serves 6-8

1 5½ oz. box au gratin potatoes   **2 T. minced dried onion**

1. Cook according to directions on box adding 2 T. minced onions to liquid.

Celebration Slaw

Prepare ahead! The longer it stands, the better it tastes!
(Keeps up to three weeks)

Preparation time: 25 minutes   Serves 10-12

Slaw

1 large head cabbage	**1 small onion**
1 green pepper	**2 carrots**

Dressing

1 cup sugar	**1 t. celery seed**
1 t. salt	**1 cup corn or safflower oil**
1 t. dry mustard	**1 cup cider vinegar**

1. Shred cabbage, green pepper, onion, and carrots.
2. Toss in a large bowl and set aside.
3. In a saucepan combine sugar, salt, mustard, celery seed, oil, and vinegar.
4. Bring to a boil and cool slightly.
5. Pour over slaw, mixing well.
6. Cover and refrigerate.

Note: Without a fast method to shred cabbage, buy pre-shredded cabbage from the grocery.

To Shred in Blender: Cut 1 head of cabbage into very small sections. Put ¼ of cut cabbage into blender and fill to top with water. Push chop button and let run 2-3 seconds or until cabbage is coarsely chopped. Pour into colander and drain. Repeat. CAUTION: Be sure cabbage is WELL DRAINED before adding dressing.

Hot French Bread

see p. 54

Ice Cold Watermelon

Fill a tub with cracked ice and chill whole watermelon
for several hours.
If refrigerator space is available, cut melon into wedges,
wrap in plastic wrap, and chill until ready to serve.
Eat in hand or on paper plates.

Menu IV
Three Cheers for the Fourth of July

Flags — balloons — red, white, and blue paper cloths and napkins!

Bucket Fried Chicken
Beans and Chili
Escalloped Pineapple
Crusty Cheese Loaf
Mile High Strawberry Pie
Cold Beer…Chilled Wines…Iced Tea

Bucket Fried Chicken

Preparation time: ZERO

There are a wide choice of restaurants and carry-outs that specialize in bucket fried chicken. Allow 2 to 3 pieces of chicken per person, cautioning the restaurant not to fill the bucket with backs and wings.

Beans and Chili

(a sure picnic hit . . . hearty and different)

Preparation time: 10 minutes   Cooking time: 1 hour

Serves 16-20

2 16 oz. cans Boston style baked beans, undrained

2 16 oz. cans red kidney beans New Orleans style, drained

2 15 oz. cans plain chili con carne without beans

4 t. dried minced onions

1 10 oz. box frozen yellow corn

1 cup chili sauce

1 t. Worcestershire sauce

¼ t. Tabasco

1 T. minced dried green pepper (optional)

1. Preheat oven to 350 degrees.
2. Mix all ingredients together well.
3. Pour into bean pot or oven proof bowl.
4. Cook 1 hour at 350 degrees.

Note: Can be made 2-3 days ahead and refrigerated. Freezes well.

Escalloped Pineapple

Preparation time: 7 minutes   Cooking time: 35-45 minutes
Serves 6-8 (doubles and triples well)

1 20 oz. can crushed pineapple, undrained

3 cups white bread torn into small pieces, crusts removed

2 eggs

1 t. vanilla

1½ cups sugar

1 cup Half and Half (milk and cream)

1. Preheat oven to 350 degrees.
2. Cut crusts off bread and tear into small pieces.
3. Beat eggs with whisk—20 seconds.
4. Combine undrained pineapple, bread, Half and Half, eggs, vanilla, and sugar in well buttered casserole.
5. Stir to mix well. Mixture will look soupy.
6. Bake 350 degrees 35-45 minutes or until pineapple is the consistency of mashed potatoes.

Note: Can be made a day or two ahead of time except for adding bread at last minute.

Crusty Cheese Loaf

Preparation time: 10 minutes   Cooking time: 15 minutes
Serves 12 heartily

1 loaf French bread (12″ long)

½ cup butter, softened to room temperature

2 5 oz. jars sharp cheese spread

2 T. minced parsley (optional)

1. Preheat oven to 350 degrees.
2. Cut bread lengthwise down center. Do not cut through bottom crust.
3. Make 8 slices crosswise, not cutting through bottom crust.
4. Mix cheese, butter, parsley together until well blended.
5. Spread generously between slices and over top of loaf.
6. Tie string around loaf to hold it together.
7. Bake unwrapped, 15 minutes at 350 degrees — or until cheese is melted and bread is crusty.
8. Wrap in foil to keep warm.

Mile-High Strawberry Pie

SEE DESSERT CHAPTER, P. 218

EVERYBODY LOVES A GALA

The Do-It-Ahead Cocktail Buffet

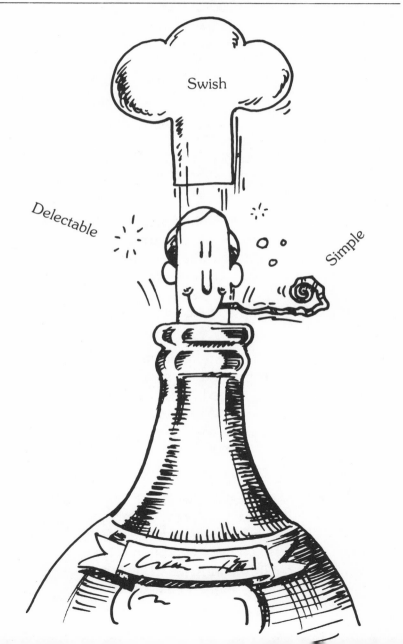

EVERYBODY LOVES A GALA

The Bar

Whatever the set-up, conviviality begins at the bar whether it be an impressive built-in or a card table covered with a brightly colored cloth or sheet.

Though popular drinks vary with region and season, basics are: Bourbon, Scotch, Vodka, Gin, and Rum. Add a bottle or two of chilled red and white wine. And then the mixes: club soda, tonic, Tom Collins, ginger ale, Seven Up, and, also, some lemon peel and green unstuffed olives.

For non-drinkers and calorie counters there are the tonic water and sodas served with a twist of lemon peel over ice, plus delectable juices galore.

Fill a large ice chest with ice and slide under the table or beside an improvised bar along with extra bottles. Bar "musts" are: ice bucket full of ice, large pitcher of ice water, highball glasses, wine glasses, jigger glasses, and spoons for stirring.

Count on average guest having three drinks.

18-24 drinks	allow 2 fifths
20-40 drinks	allow 3 fifths
Wine	3 bottles will yield 16 glasses of wine in a 4 oz. glass

Menu I

Raw Oysters on Crushed Ice

Cocktail Sauce

Imperial Crab Fluff

with

Melba Toast

Garden Fresh Vegetable Tray

Rolled Stuffed Salami

Cheese Cake

Coffee

Raw Oysters on Crushed Ice

Preparation time: 10 minutes   Serves 8-10

1-2 qts. large,   **Crushed ice**
juicy oysters

1. Drain oysters and pat dry with paper towel.
2. On large glass, or other attractive platter, make bed of firmly crushed ice.
3. Fit small glass bowl of cocktail sauce into center.
4. Surround with oysters and parsley sprigs.
5. Beside platter, place container of festive toothpicks for spearing oysters and dipping into sauce.

Cocktail Sauce

Preparation time: 4 minutes   Makes 1¼ cups

1 12 oz. bottle Chili sauce   **⅛ t. coarsely ground black**
1 T. bottled lemon juice   **pepper**
¼ t. salt   **2 t. horseradish**
                             ¼ t. Tabasco

1. Mix all ingredients together until thoroughly blended.
2. Pour into glass bowl, cover and refrigerate until ready to serve.

Imperial Crab Fluff

Preparation time: 30 minutes
(subtract 10 minutes if crab shells removed and cheese grated)
Cooking time: 20 minutes
Serves 12-15

1 lb. fresh select crab meat
¼ cup bottled lemon juice
1 8 oz. carton (1 cup) sour cream
2 cups grated Swiss cheese (flavor better if buy in bulk and grate at home)
4 T. butter

4 T. blended flour (sauce and gravy flour)
2 cups whole milk
1 egg yolk
½ t. salt
½ t. Worcestershire Sauce
½ t. Tabasco
2 T. dry white wine
White Melba toast

1. Go through crab meat and carefully remove any shells. Sprinkle with ¼ cup bottled lemon juice, and refrigerate until ready to use.
2. Make basic cream sauce in large frying pan (or double boiler which will hold 8 cups) on top of stove. Melt butter and blend in flour. Add milk, stirring with wire whisk constantly until thoroughly blended.
3. Add grated Swiss cheese.
4. Add 1 beaten egg yolk, mixing well.
5. Add salt, Worcestershire Sauce, Tabasco and wine, tasting to correct seasoning.
6. Stir in sour cream, mixing well. Put cover on pan and set aside until ready to add crab.
7. Lastly, add crab, heating on lowest heat until mixture is heated throughout.
8. Pour in chafing dish over hot water, or in serving dish on electric hot plate.
9. Surround with white Melba toast and serve.

Garden Fresh Vegetable Tray

(prepare the day before . . . choose at least four of the following)

4 or 5 choices will serve 8

1 head cauliflower, separated into flowerettes

1 bunch broccoli, flowerettes only

½ lb. button mushrooms

2 green peppers, cut into thin strips

1 small bunch carrots, cut into sticks

1 pint cherry tomatoes, stemmed

2 medium sized zucchini, thinly sliced

1 bunch celery, cut into sticks

Parsley for garnish

1. Wash all vegetables and drain well.
2. Separate cauliflower and broccoli into flowerettes.
3. Cut green peppers into strips.
4. Clean carrots and celery and cut into sticks.
5. Stem tomatoes and mushrooms.
6. Store in airtight containers in refrigerator until ready to use.
7. At serving time, cluster vegetables on an attractive tray, placing glass bowl of dip in center. Garnish liberally with parsley.

Dip for Fresh Vegetables

(see p. 14 for other dips)

Preparation time: 5 minutes   Makes 2 cups

1 8 oz. package cream cheese, softened

1 cup mayonnaise (no substitutes)

1 1 oz. package Hidden Valley Ranch Style Salad Dressing Mix

1. Combine all ingredients and mix well with fork until thoroughly blended.
2. Put in serving dish, sprinkle with paprika, cover tightly, and refrigerate until ready to use.

Rolled Stuffed Salami

(refrigerates well — make day before)

Preparation time: 20 minutes   Serves 8 (makes 28)

2 4 oz. boxes Hormel Party Salami (or equivalent amount of any thin sliced, cooked salami)
Party toothpicks with frills
1 8 oz. package cream cheese, softened

3 t. horseradish
2½ t. lemon juice
2½ T. mayonnaise
1 chopped green pepper (optional)

1. Combine softened cream cheese, horseradish, lemon juice, mayonnaise, and green pepper in small mixing bowl.
2. Mix with fork until well combined.
3. Spread each salami slice with heaping teaspoon of cream cheese mixture.
4. Roll up and secure with toothpick.
5. Cover tightly with foil and refrigerate.
6. At serving time, place on tray and garnish with parsley.

Cheesecake

Buy from local deli or use Sara Lee from frozen food counter.

Menu II

Ham Biscuits with Mustard Mayonnaise

Oyster-Clam Casserole

with

Melba Toast

Spiced Cheese Chutney Mold

Assorted Crackers

Pineapple-Green Cherry Spears

Coffee

OYSTER ∽CLAM   CASSEROLE

Ham Biscuits with Mustard Mayonnaise

Preparation time: 20 minutes   Serves 8-10

Three dozen 2 inch round bakery biscuits
2 lbs. thinly sliced ham*

1 bunch parsley
Mustard mayonnaise

1. Order ahead or buy and freeze biscuits.
2. Split biscuits and spread with mustard mayonnaise.
3. Add generous 2 inch slivers of ham and put top on each biscuit.
4. Arrange on two medium-sized platters or trays.
5. Cover with dampened dish towel, wrap securely in plastic wrap and place in refrigerator until ready to serve.
6. Garnish with parsley.
7. Place one platter on buffet table, reserving second for replenishment.

* Well-flavored ham can be bought at delicatessen and sliced to order, or purchased in can or loaf and sliced at grocery or home. Recommended brands are: Wilson, Hormel, Swift, and Masterpiece.

Mustard Mayonnaise

Preparation time: 7 minutes   Makes 2 cups

3 T. dry mustard
2 T. cider vinegar
⅛ t. Tabasco

½ t. horseradish
2 cups mayonnaise (no substitutes)

1. Dissolve mustard in vinegar.
2. Add Tabasco and horseradish.
3. Blend in mayonnaise and mix well.

Oyster-Clam Casserole with Melba Toast

(easy to put together)

Preparation time: 15 minutes   Serves 8-10

1 qt. stewing oysters (4 cups including liquid)

2 cans Snow's Clam Chowder, undiluted

2 drops Tabasco

1 t. Worcestershire

¼ t. salt

¼ t. ground black pepper

1 stick butter

2 cups Pepperidge Farm Cube Stuffing Herb Seasoned

2 packages white Melba Toast

1. Drain oysters, reserving liquid.
2. In a mixing bowl, combine oyster liquid, Clam Chowder, Tabasco, Worcestershire, salt, and pepper. Stir until well mixed.
3. Butter two 1½ qt. casseroles (or one 3 qt.).*
4. Cover bottom of each casserole dish with a fourth of oysters, a fourth of soup mixture, topped with a fourth (½ cup) of cube stuffing. Dot each layer with 2 T. butter. Repeat layers ending up with ½ cup cube stuffing over top.
5. At party time, place in 350 degree oven and cook 15-20 minutes or until piping hot. CAUTION — DO NOT OVERCOOK! (Should be of consistency to dribble on Melba Toast with medium size serving spoon.)
6. Transfer to chafing dish or hot plate to keep warm on buffet table. Surround with Melba Toast.

* Better to have two dishes for oysters than one. While one dish is being served, other can be cooking and will stay hot in warm oven.

Spiced Cheese Chutney Mold

Preparation time: 12 minutes   Serves 12-14

1 8 oz. package cream cheese, softened

3 cups grated sharp Cheddar cheese (3 4 oz. packages)

3 T. green onion tops, chopped fine

¼ t. Tabasco

¼ t. curry powder

2 T. dry sherry

1 6 oz. jar chutney (Major Grey's preferred)

minced parsley for top

1. Grease a 9 inch pie pan. Set aside.
2. Combine softened cream cheese, Cheddar cheese, onion tops, Tabasco, curry powder, and sherry in a mixing bowl.
3. Mix until ingredients are well combined and smooth.
4. Press cheese mixture into pie pan and refrigerate until firm — at least 1 hour.
5. Unmold on serving platter.
6. Spread top and sides of mold with chutney (approximately ½ bottle).
7. Sprinkle minced parsley over top.
8. Serve with assorted crackers.

Pineapple-Green Cherry Spears

Preparation time: 10 minutes   Serves 10-12

**1 20 oz. can of pineapple
chunks**
**2 small bottles green
Maraschino cherries**

2½ T. light rum
Festive toothpicks

1. Drain pineapple and cherries, patting dry with paper towel.
2. Put in mixing bowl, toss with 2½ T. light rum. Cover and refrigerate for 2-3 hours.
3. Before serving drain rum from pineapple and cherries.
4. On festive toothpicks alternate 2 pineapple chunks and 1 cherry until all have been used.
5. Arrange on serving platter, cover with plastic wrap and refrigerate until party time.

Menu III

Shrimp Mousse

Polynesian Sweet and Sour Meat Balls

Roquefort Cheese Ring

Assorted Crackers

Potpourri of Fresh Fruit

with

Creme of Liqueur Almond

Coffee

Shrimp Mousse

(see rule for congealed salads, p. 238)

Preparation time: 18 minutes
Serves 10-12 (or 30 if spread on crackers)

1 lb. cooked, peeled, and deveined shrimp

3 envelopes plain gelatin

1 14½ oz. can Swanson's Chicken Broth

1 10¾ oz. can Cream of Shrimp soup

1 8 oz. package cream cheese, softened

½ t. Tabasco

3 T. bottled lemon juice

½ t. salt

1 green onion chopped in 4 pieces

1 8 oz. carton sour cream

1 cup celery, chopped fine

olives, pimento, and parsley for garnish

1. Chop coarsely one half of the shrimp (¼ to ½ inches each piece). Set aside.
2. Pour one half can of Chicken Broth into saucepan and heat on medium high.
3. Sprinkle gelatin on remainder of Chicken Broth in can to soften.
4. Add gelatin mixture to hot Chicken Broth, stir until dissolved, and remove from heat.
5. Place in blender: remainder of shrimp (unchopped), shrimp soup, cream cheese, Tabasco, lemon juice, salt, green onion, and Chicken Broth gelatin mixture.
6. Blend on high until all ingredients are thoroughly combined, pouring half of mixture into mixing bowl.
7. Add sour cream to mixture in blender. Blend and pour into mixing bowl with other half of blended mousse.
8. Stir until well combined.
9. Fold in chopped celery and chopped shrimp.
10. Pour mixture into lightly oiled 1½ qt. mold, or round bowl.
11. Cover and refrigerate until firm.
12. Unmold on round platter, surround with crackers, and garnish with olives, pimento strips, and parsley.

Polynesian Sweet and Sour Meatballs

(make ahead — freezes well)

Preparation and Cooking time: 55 minutes
Serves 8-10 (makes about 55 meat balls)

MEAT BALLS

1½ lbs. LEAN ground beef
¾ cup Old Fashioned Quaker Oats
1 8 oz. can sliced water chestnuts, drained and finely chopped
½ cup milk
1 egg, slightly beaten
¼ t. garlic powder

¼ t. ginger
1 t. Accent
½ t. onion salt
¼ t. salt
¼ t. Tabasco
1 T. Soy Sauce

1. Mix all ingredients together well until thoroughly combined.
2. Form into balls about 1 inch to 1¼ inch.
3. When enough meat balls are ready for frying pan, brown first batch while continuing to make next amount.
4. Brown on medium low heat in a covered skillet, approximately 3 minutes on each side
5. Drain well.

continued on next page

Sauce

1 15½ oz. can crushed pineapple

1 7½ oz. can crushed pineapple, drained

1 firmly packed cup light brown sugar

1 cup beef bouillon (Swanson's preferred)

½ cup red wine vinegar

2 T. cornstarch

1 cup chopped green pepper (optional)

1. Drain 15½ oz. can crushed pineapple, reserving juice (should yield 1 cup).
2. Combine pineapple juice and brown sugar in 6 qt. pan.
3. Add bouillon and red wine vinegar.
4. Stir in 2 T. cornstarch and whisk until thoroughly dissolved.
5. Bring to rolling boil, reduce heat, and cook until slightly thickened, stirring constantly (approximately 8 minutes).
6. Drain 7½ oz. can pineapple.
7. Add both cans drained pineapple, green pepper, and meat balls.
8. Simmer in sauce until thoroughly heated through — approximately 10-12 minutes.
9. Transfer to chafing dish or heated bowl.

   (Furnish guests with toothpicks for spearing meat balls)

Roquefort Cheese Ring

Preparation time: 12 minutes   Serves 8-10

**1 8 oz. package cream
cheese, softened**

**4 oz. (or 1 cup) crumbled
Bleu or Roquefort cheese**

1 8 oz. carton sour cream

1 t. salt

¼ t. bottled lemon juice

1 T. dry white wine

½ cup cold water

**1 envelope Knox plain
gelatin**

paprika

1. Soften gelatin in ½ cup cold water. Place over boiling water to melt.
2. Blend cream cheese, Roquefort, sour cream, salt, lemon juice, and wine either by hand or in blender.
3. Add gelatin and mix thoroughly.
4. Pour into lightly oiled ring mold.
5. Cover and refrigerate until set.
6. Unmold on serving tray, garnish with parsley, sprinkle lightly with paprika, and serve with assorted crackers.

Potpourri of Fresh Fruit
with Crème of Liqueur Almond
Serves 8

Choose 5-6 fruits from the following:

3 tart apples, sliced into wedges

4 ripe pears, cut into slices

1 qt. strawberries, stemmed

2 lbs. grapes, cut in clusters

1 lb. dates, seeded

1 lb. dried figs

1 16 oz. can pineapple chunks or

1 fresh pineapple cut into chunks

1 large canteloupe, cut into small slices or melon balls

5 fresh apricots, cut into slices

toothpicks for dipping fruit

1. Select fruits, wash, draining fresh and canned, and cut into appropriate sizes.
2. Place fruit in separate containers, saturate with Fruit Fresh syrup (see following recipe), cover tightly with plastic wrap, and refrigerate until ready to use.
3. At serving time, cluster fruit attractively on large platter. Place glass compote or glass dish of Crème of Liqueur Almond in center for dipping fruit.

Fruit Fresh Syrup

(for preserving fresh fruits)

(makes enough for 1 qt. of fruit)

2 t. Fruit Fresh　　　　　**3 T. water**

1. Dissolve Fruit Fresh in water and toss with 1 quart of fruit.
2. Refrigerate in air tight containers until ready to use.
3. At serving time, drain any syrup or accumulated liquid from fruit.

continued on next page

Crème of Liqueur Almond

(make in advance — keeps well for a month)

Preparation time: 10 minutes   Makes 2 cups

2 cups sour cream
6 T. powdered sugar

**2 T. almond liqueur
(Amaretto, etc.)**

1. Combine sour cream, powdered sugar, and almond liqueur.
2. Stir to blend well.
3. Cover and refrigerate in serving dish.
4. At serving time, place bowl in center of Potpourri Fruit Tray. Garnish with fresh mint sprigs if available.

Menu IV

Salmon Mousse

with

Cucumber and Horseradish Sauce

Assorted Stuffed Eggs and Dill Pickles

Mock Pizza

Broccoli-Spinach Dip

Orange Nectar Cake

Coffee

Salmon Mousse

(if made a day or two in advance — flavor improves)

Preparation time: 20 minutes   Serves 8-10

3 cups red salmon (15½ oz. can makes 2 cups; 7½ oz. can makes 1 cup)

1 can Campbell's Cream of Shrimp soup, undiluted

1 cup finely chopped celery

1 cup sour cream (8 oz. container)

2 t. minced dried chives

1 t. dry mustard

½ t. Worcestershire Sauce

½ t. horseradish

6 T. bottled lemon juice

¼ t. Tabasco

¼ t. salt

3 envelopes unflavored gelatin

½ cup cold water

1 cup boiling water

tray of Rye Crisp crackers (optional)

1. Drain salmon.
2. Remove skin and bones from salmon and place in large mixing bowl.
3. Add seasonings: chives, mustard, Worcestershire, horse-radish, lemon juice, Tabasco, and salt, mixing well.
4. In separate bowl sprinkle gelatin over ½ cup cold water and allow to stand 2-3 minutes to soften.
5. Add 1 cup boiling water and thoroughly dissolve gelatin. Set aside.
6. Fold sour cream and Cream of Shrimp soup into salmon mixture.
7. Add chopped celery.
8. Combine gelatin and salmon mixture, mixing well.
9. Turn into an 8 cup fish mold, oblong, or oval mold and place in refrigerator to set.
10. When ready to serve, garnish with cucumber slices and parsley and serve with rye crisp crackers.

Cucumber and Horseradish Sauce

Preparation time: 8 minutes   Makes 1¼ cups

1 cup sour cream (1 8 oz. carton)

¼ cup mayonnaise

1 small cucumber (approximately heaping ½ cup)

2 t. horseradish

¼ t. salt

1. Peel cucumber and remove seeds. Chop coarsely and put in blender.
2. Add sour cream, mayonnaise, horseradish, and salt.
3. Run blender until all ingredients are thoroughly mixed.
4. Pour into serving bowl, cover tightly, and refrigerate until cold and sauce thickens — approximately 1-2 hours.
5. At serving time, sprinkle with paprika and serve with Salmon Mousse.

Assorted Stuffed Eggs and Dill Pickles

(see rule for hard cooked eggs, p. 238)

Preparation time: 20 minutes   Makes 24 egg halves

12 hard cooked eggs
4 T. mayonnaise (no substitutes)
1 t. dry mustard
2 T. plus 2 t. cider vinegar

½ t. salt
pimento strips, anchovies, ripe olives, for garnish
1 20 oz. jar dill pickle spears

1. Remove shells from eggs and slice lengthwise.
2. Carefully remove yolks with a spoon and place in mixing bowl.
3. Mash yolks with a fork until fine.
4. Add mayonnaise, mustard, vinegar, and salt to egg yolks.
5. Beat by hand or in electric mixer until all ingredients are well combined and mixture is light and fluffy.
6. Carefully mound mixture into egg whites.
7. Sprinkle lightly with paprika and vary with the following garnishes: pimento strips, anchovies, and ripe olives.
8. Cover tightly with plastic wrap and refrigerate.
9. At serving time, arrange attractively on platter, interspersing with dill pickle slices and sprigs of parsley.

Mock Pizza

(do ahead and bake at last minute)

Preparation time: 12 minutes   Makes 24 servings

6 whole English muffins
Softened butter (approximately 12 t.)
36 2" diameter pieces thin sliced salami (or equivalent amount of larger pieces of salami, approximately 15 slices)

3 cups (12 oz.) shredded Romano (or Mozzarella) cheese
1 10½ can Chef Boy-ar-dee Pizza Sauce with Cheese
12 heaping t. Parmesan cheese

1. Preheat oven to 350 degrees if baking immediately.
2. Halve English muffins and lay on cookie sheet.
3. Lightly butter muffins (1 t. per half).
4. Run under broiler until just barely browned, approximately 3 minutes.
5. Use 3 whole pieces of 2" diameter salami per muffin half. Cut thin slices in fourths.
6. Place salami on muffin halves and top each half with 2 heaping T. shredded Romano (or Mozzarella) cheese.
7. Dribble 1 T. pizza sauce over each muffin.
8. Sprinkle liberally (approximately 1 heaping t.) with Parmesan cheese.
9. If not baking immediately, cover and set aside.
10. At serving time, bake 10 minutes at 350 degrees.
11. Cut each muffin in half or fourths, arrange attractively on serving tray, and garnish with parsley.

Broccoli-Spinach Dip

(make 2 or 3 days ahead or freeze)

Preparation time: 12 minutes   Makes 4 cups

1 10 oz. package frozen chopped broccoli, thawed and well drained

1 10 oz. package frozen chopped spinach, thawed and well drained

2 cups sour cream

5 heaping T. Knorr dry leek soup mix, (approximately ¾ package)

2 small green onions, tops included

1 t. dill weed

1 t. Good Season's Italian Salad Dressing Mix

¼ t. Tabasco

1 T. dried minced parsley

1 pinch garlic powder

1 cup mayonnaise (no substitutes)

1 large package Frito dip chips

1. Place drained broccoli, spinach, sour cream, soup mix, onions, dill weed, dry salad mix, Tabasco, minced parsley, and garlic powder in blender.
2. Blend until thoroughly mixed. Stir mixture down and re-blend several times.
3. Add mayonnaise and continue blending until all ingredients are well combined and smooth.
4. Cover and refrigerate until ready to use.
5. At serving time, pour into glass bowl, sprinkle lightly with paprika, and surround with dip sized Fritos.

ORANGE NECTAR CAKE

SEE DESSERT CHAPTER, P. 223

Menu V
"Last Minute Wonders from the Deli"

Skewered Appetizer Kabobs

Succulent Assorted Cold Cuts

Potato Rolls and Party Rye

Mayonnaise. . .Mustard Mayonnaise

Cheese Tray with Apple Slices and Grapes

French Pastries

Coffee

Skewered Appetizer Kabobs

Preparation time: 15 minutes   Serves 8
(allowing 3 per person)

1 bottle green olives
**1 small bottle miniature
  sweet gherkins**
1 bottle pickled onions

24 marinated shrimp
**24 decorative cocktail
  toothpicks, with colored
  frills**

1. Drain olives, pickles, and onions.
2. Spear 1 olive, shrimp, pickle, and onion (in order) on each toothpick.
3. Arrange on serving tray, decorate with parsley, and place on buffet table.

Succulent Assorted Cold Cuts

Choose at least 2 or more meats, allowing ⅛ lb. meat per person, per sandwich

Corned beef, thinly sliced
Rare roast of beef,
  thinly sliced
Ham, thinly sliced
Turkey (or smoked turkey),
  thinly sliced

1 head curly endive
Potato rolls
  (allow 2 per person)
1-2 loaves Party rye bread

1. On large serving tray arrange meat attractively. Garnish with curly endive.
2. Place potato rolls and rye bread in bread trays or baskets beside serving tray.
3. Serve with choice of mayonnaise and mustard mayonnaise.

Mustard Mayonnaise

Preparation time: 7 minutes   Makes 2 cups

3 T. dry mustard
2 T. cider vinegar
⅛ t. Tabasco

½ t. horseradish
2 cups mayonnaise
  (no substitutes)

1. Dissolve mustard in vinegar.
2. Add Tabasco and horseradish.
3. Blend in mayonnaise and mix well.

Cheese Tray with Apple Slices and Grapes

(prepare cheese tray ahead of time and add fruit at last minute. Cheese should be at room temperature for full flavor)

Preparation time: 15 minutes   Serves 8-10

2-3 tart apples
2 lbs. seedless grapes
 (purple and green)
4-6 oz. Brie (Bree)*
4-6 oz. Bel Paese
 (bel-pay-ay-ze)*

4-6 oz. aged Cheddar*
Assortment of Melba Toast
 and thin crisp crackers
Fruit Fresh

1. Cut apples into wedges, sprinkle with FRUIT FRESH (see below), wrap tightly in plastic wrap and refrigerate until ready to serve.
2. Wash and dry grapes. Cut into small clusters. Refrigerate until ready to use.
3. Arrange cheese attractively on tray with apples and clusters of grapes placed among cheese.
4. Put Melba Toast and crackers in baskets on each side of tray.

* These are only suggestions. Ask your Deli to help with selections, but always choose a soft, a semi-soft, and a semi-firm to firm cheese for variety.

Fruit Fresh

(for preserving fresh fruit)

2 t. Fruit Fresh　　　　**3 T. water**

1. Dissolve Fruit Fresh in water and toss with apples.
2. Wrap tightly in plastic wrap or put in airtight container and refrigerate until ready to use.

French Pasteries

Glamorous to the eye and scrumptious to the taste are a colorful assortment of French pastries available from the Deli or bakery. (allow 1½ pastries per guest)

TOP OF THE MORNING WEEKEND BRUNCH

The Intimate Few or a Bunch

TOP OF THE MORNING WEEKEND BRUNCH

Hot Tamale Cheese Casserole
Tangy Apricot Salad Mold
Mexican Cornbread
Coffee

Never-Fail Mock Cheese Soufflé
Hot Fruit Compote
Asparagus Vinaigrette
with
Pimento Strips
Gingerbread-Raisin Muffins
Coffee

Tuna Mushroom Party Eggs
Bloody Mary Tomato Aspic Salad
Yellow Cling Peach Halves
with
Currant Jelly
Blueberry Muffins
Coffee

California Sausage Bake
Top of the Morning Fruit Salad
Toasted English Muffins
Coffee

Icy Cold Cucumber Soup
Springtime-Summery Fruit Melange
with
Lime Sherbet
Piquant Fruit Salad Dressing
Party Ham Sandwiches
Iced Tea

Drinks

Whether buffet or seated, the merry mood sets in with an imaginative choice of drinks at an improvised bar. Take your pick!

(see Cocktail Buffet, p. __161__ for bar information)

Bloody Mary

(the most popular "getter-upper")

Serves 6

1 24 oz. bottle Bloody Mary mix, (Mr. & Mrs. T. preferred)
6 oz. vodka

¼ t. Tabasco
¼ t. Worcestershire Sauce
Celery sticks or lime quarters for garnish

1. Pour bloody mary mix, vodka, Tabasco, and Worcestershire Sauce in pitcher. Stir well to mix.
2. Cover and chill in refrigerator until ready to serve.
3. Serve over ice and garnish with celery sticks or quartered limes.

Screwdriver

Serves 6

4 cups orange juice
6 oz. vodka

Ice
Thin slices of orange (optional)

1. Put 2 or 3 cubes of ice into highball glass.
2. Add 1 oz. vodka per glass.
3. Fill balance of glass with orange juice and stir.
4. Garnish each glass with thin slice of orange.

Milk Punch

(the brunch standby)

(flavor best when made 3-4 hours or a day in advance)

Serves 4-6

2 cups milk
1 cup Half and Half
(cream and milk)
½ cup brandy

6 T. dark rum
3½ T. granulated sugar
Freshly grated nutmeg
(optional)

1. Combine milk, Half and Half, brandy, rum, and sugar in pitcher.
2. Stir until sugar is dissolved and all ingredients are well combined.
3. Cover and refrigerate until well chilled — preferably 3-4 hours.
4. Serve over ice and garnish with freshly grated nutmeg.

Spritzer

Serves 8-10

1 bottle chilled Rhine wine
or Sauterne
Soda water

Ice cubes
Lemon slices

1. Pour 3 oz. chilled wine into each highball or wine glass along with ice cubes.
2. Fill balance with soda water, stir gently and garnish with lemon slice.

For the Non-Drinkers V-8 Cocktail

(hard to beat and found on all grocery shelves)

Pour over ice and garnish with a celery stalk.

Virgin Mary

Serves 6

1 24 oz. bottle Bloody Mary mix, (Mr. & Mrs. T. preferred)
¼ t. Tabasco

¼ t. Worcestershire Sauce
Celery sticks or lime quarters for garnish

1. Pour Bloody Mary mix, Tabasco, and Worcestershire Sauce in pitcher. Stir well to mix.
2. Cover and chill in refrigerator until ready to serve.
3. Serve over ice and garnish with celery sticks or quartered limes.

Mock Pink Champagne

(tasty and champagne-like, but non-spirit)

Serves 8-10

1 cup sugar
1 cup water
1 cup canned grapefruit juice

1 cup orange juice
⅓ cup grenadine syrup*
1 qt. ginger ale, chilled

1. Boil sugar and water together for 5 minutes.
2. Cool and pour into large pitcher.
3. Add grapefruit and orange juice. Stir well and refrigerate until well chilled.
4. When ready to serve, add grenadine syrup* and chilled gingerale.
5. Stir and serve over ice.

* Available at liquor store or gourmet shop

Menu I

Hot Tamale Cheese Casserole

Tangy Apricot Salad Mold

Cream Cheese Dressing

Mexican Cornbread

Coffee

Hot Tamale Cheese Casserole

Preparation time: 10 minutes   Cooking time: 12 minutes
Serves 4 heartily (allows 3 tamales each; double for eight)

2 13½ oz. jars beef tamales with sauce, (Hormel's preferred)

1 can Cream of Mushroom soup, undiluted

1 t. Taco seasoning

½ cup tamale sauce (drained from jar)

1 4 oz. package grated sharp Cheddar cheese

1. Preheat oven to 425 degrees
2. Open tamales and drain sauce into mixing bowl.
3. Remove paper from tamales and lay in bottom of 8×8 Pyrex dish (or oven proof baking dish).
4. Mix together: sauce, soup, and Taco seasoning, stirring until well blended.
5. Pour sauce over tamales.
6. Sprinkle grated cheese evenly over top.
7. Bake 425 degrees 12 minutes or until cheese is melted and tamales are heated through.

Tangy Apricot Salad Mold

(see rule for congealing salads, p. __238__)

Preparation time: 12 minutes
Makes 10 individual molds or 1½ qt. mold

**1 6 oz. (or 2 3 oz.)
package apricot jello**

1 cup orange juice

2 cups buttermilk

**1 15¼ oz. can crushed
pineapple, drained**

**2 16 oz. cans apricot
halves, drained***

1 cup broken pecan pieces

**1 6 oz. bottle green
Maraschino cherries**

1. Heat orange juice in saucepan until hot.
2. Add jello to hot orange juice. Stir until dissolved. Set aside.
3. Cut 1 can drained apricot halves into fourths. Add to orange juice – jello mixture.
4. Stir in 2 cups buttermilk.
5. Fold in drained crushed pineapple and nuts.
6. Pour into oiled mold and chill until firm.
7. To serve, unmold on bed of lettuce, surround with second can of drained apricot halves and green cherries placed in center of each apricot half.
8. Serve with cream cheese dressing.

* Reserve second can of apricots for garnish.

Cream Cheese Dressing

Preparation time: 6 minutes   Makes 1 cup

**1 3 oz. package cream
cheese, softened**

**½ cup mayonnaise
(no substitutes)**

1 T. milk

salt to taste

**1 t. bottled lemon juice
(optional)**

1. Mix cream cheese, mayonnaise, and milk together until well blended.
2. Add dash of salt and lemon juice. Beat by hand until light and fluffy.
3. Refrigerate until ready to serve.

Mexican Cornbread

Preparation time: 8 minutes   Cooking time: 35 minutes
Makes 30 small squares

1 15 oz. package corn muffin mix (Dromedary preferred)

1 egg

1 8 oz. carton sour cream

½ t. salt

1 16 oz. can cream style corn, drained

1 3 oz. can mild green chopped chilies, drained

⅔ cup salad oil

1 4 oz. package grated sharp Cheddar cheese (or 1 cup)

¼ t. Tabasco (for those who like hot seasoning)

1. Preheat oven to 425 degrees.
2. Grease a 9×12 baking dish.
3. Mix together: muffin mix, egg, sour cream, salt, corn, chilies, salad oil, and one half of the cheese.
4. Beat by hand until well blended — about 50 strokes. Batter will be lumpy.
5. Pour into baking dish and top with remaining cheese.
6. Bake 425 degrees for 35 minutes or until top is golden and batter tests with a toothpick or wire tester.
7. Cool 15 minutes before slicing.

Note: This can be made ahead and frozen.

Menu II

Never-Fail Mock Cheese Souffle′

Hot Fruit Compote

Asparagus Vinaigrette with Pimento Strips

Gingerbread-Raisin Muffins

Coffee

Never-Fail Mock Cheese Soufflé

(the do-it-ahead soufflé)

Preparation time: 15 minutes   Cooking time: 40-45 minutes
Serves 8

1 loaf French bread, sliced	**2 t. Worcestershire Sauce**
3 cups grated sharp Cheddar cheese	**½ t. curry powder**
2 cups milk	**½ cup sherry**
4 eggs	**butter for bread**
1 t. salt	**1 2 oz. package slivered almonds**

1. Remove crusts from bread, butter each slice generously, and slice in half.
2. Place half bread slices tightly in buttered 9×13 baking dish.
3. Top with half of grated cheese. (1½ cups)
4. Cover with remaining bread slices and top with remainder of cheese.
5. Combine milk, eggs, salt, Worcestershire, curry powder, and sherry, mixing well.
6. Pour liquid mixture over cheese and bread.
7. Cover tightly and refrigerate overnight.
8. When ready to bake, preheat oven to 350 degrees.
9. Sprinkle top of soufflé with almonds and place uncovered in shallow pan of water. (a cookie sheet with a small amount of water will hold this size dish)
10. Bake 350 degrees for 40-45 minutes or until top is golden brown and soufflé is puffy.

Hot Fruit Compote

Preparation time: 12 minutes   Serves 8

1 16 oz. can peach halves
1 16 oz. can pineapple
chunks
1 16 oz. can apricot halves
1 16 oz. seedless Bing
cherries
2½ T. cornstarch
¼ cup water

1 cup brown sugar
6 T. butter
½ t. curry powder
½ t. nutmeg
½ cup sherry
sour cream

1. Preheat oven to 325 degrees.
2. Drain all fruit well.
3. Lightly butter a 3 quart baking dish.
4. Dissolve 2½ T. cornstarch in ¼ cup water.
5. Melt brown sugar and butter in saucepan. Add curry powder and nutmeg.
6. Stir in cornstarch mixture and cook over medium heat, stirring constantly until thickened.
7. Add sherry and stir until well mixed.
8. Place drained fruit attractively in baking dish and spoon thickened sauce evenly over top of fruit.
9. Bake 25-30 minutes or until fruit is bubbling and hot.
10. At serving time, sprinkle lightly with paprika and spoon dollops of sour cream over top of fruit.

Asparagus Vinaigrette with Pimento Strips

Preparation time: 10 minutes   Serves 8
Vinaigrette dressing makes 1¼ cups

**2 15 oz. cans all green
  whole asparagus spears**
1 T. Dijon mustard
1 T. bottled lemon juice
2 T. red wine vinegar
½ t. sugar

½ t. salt
½ t. pepper
½ T. chopped dried chives
**1 cup olive oil (or
  safflower or corn oil)**
1 4 oz. jar whole pimentos

1. Drain asparagus and pat dry on paper towels.
2. In a small bowl, combine 1 T. Dijon mustard, 1 T. lemon juice, 2 T. wine vinegar, ½ t. sugar, ½ t. salt, ½ t. pepper, and ½T. chopped dried chives. Stir to mix well.
3. Beat in oil slowly, whisking vigorously until dressing is smooth.
4. Spread asparagus out in shallow oblong dish.
5. Dribble 4 T. dressing over asparagus. Cover and refrigerate several hours.
6. Place remaining dressing in serving bowl, cover and refrigerate.
7. At serving time, drain asparagus and lay on bed of endive or leaf lettuce with additional dressing in center of lettuce bed.
8. Cut pimentos into thin strips and place on top of asparagus spears for garnish.
9. Let guests add additional dressing if desired.

Ginger Bread Raisin Muffins

Preparation time: 8 minutes   Makes 21 muffins

**1 box Betty Crocker
Gingerbread Mix**
1¼ cups lukewarm water
1 egg

**2 1½ oz. boxes seedless
raisins**
paper muffin liners

1. Preheat oven to 350 degrees.
2. Combine gingerbread mix, lukewarm water, and egg.
3. Stir until ingredients are well combined.
4. Stir in raisins.
5. Place paper muffin liners in muffin tin.
6. Fill each container half full.
7. Bake 350 degrees for 20 minutes or until center comes out clean when tested with a toothpick.

**Note: Freezes well. Let muffins come to room
temperature, wrap in foil, and reheat in 250
degree oven approximately 15 minutes to serve
warm.**

Menu III

Tuna Mushroom Party Eggs

Bloody Mary Tomato Aspic Salad

Yellow Cling Peach Halves

with

Currant Jelly

Blueberry Muffins

Coffee

Tuna Mushroom Party Eggs

Preparation time: 15 minutes   Cooking time: 15 minutes
Serves 8

**8 hard boiled eggs,
  peeled***

**1 13 oz. can white tuna,
  drained**

1 t. Worcestershire Sauce

½ t. bottled onion juice

¼ t. Tabasco

2 t. bottled lemon juice

**1 10¾ oz. can Cream
  of Mushroom Soup,
  undiluted**

½ t. salt

¼ t. black pepper

1 t. Dijon mustard

**2 cups grated Munster
  cheese**

**⅓ cup Half and Half
  (cream and milk)**

½ cup bread crumbs

2 T. butter

**1 8 oz. can mushrooms,
  drained**

1. Preheat oven to 425 degrees.
2. Drain tuna, run under cold water to remove any oil, and divide in half.
3. Cut eggs lengthwise. Remove yolks and mash well with fork.
4. Combine half of tuna, egg yolks, Worcestershire Sauce, onion juice, Tabasco, lemon juice, 2 T. Cream of Mushroom soup, salt, and pepper. Mix thoroughly.
5. Spoon mixture into egg whites, making fairly high mounds. Place in a lightly buttered 9×13 inch pyrex dish.
6. Combine remaining tuna, soup, mustard, cheese, Half and Half, and drained mushrooms.
7. Mix well and pour over stuffed eggs.
8. Sprinkle top with ½ cup bread crumbs and dot with small pieces butter.**
9. Cook 15 minutes 425 degrees or until dish is heated through. DO NOT OVERCOOK or egg whites will become hardened.
10. Sprinkle with paprika, garnish with parsley, and serve.

* See rule for hard-cooked eggs, p. <u>238</u>

Bloody Mary Tomato Aspic Salad

(see rule for congealing salads, p. __238__)

Preparation time: 12 minutes   Serves 8

See recipe on p. __86__

Suggested salad dressings: Sour Cream, p. __87__
Cream Cheese Mayonnaise, p. __195__

Yellow Cling Peach Halves with Currant Jelly

Preparation time: 10 minutes   Serves 8

**2 16 oz. cans yellow cling   1 12 oz. jar Red Currant
  peach halves   jelly**

1. Preheat oven to 350 degrees.
2. Drain peach halves and pat dry on paper towel.
3. Arrange peach halves in oven proof serving dish.
4. Fill center of each peach half with 1 t. Red Currant jelly.
5. Heat 10 minutes or until hot.

**Note: Can be done a day in advance and refrigerated.
      Bring to room temperature before heating.**

Blueberry Muffins

Preparation time: 8 minutes   Makes 24 individual muffins

2 13 oz. boxes blueberry muffin mix with "real" blueberries

1 16 oz. can blueberries, drained

1. Preheat oven to 400 degrees.
2. Drain well blueberries in box mix along with additional 16 oz. can of blueberries.
3. In mixing bowl, blend 2 eggs and 1 cup milk.
4. Add muffin mix and stir until just moistened.
5. Fold in blueberries.
6. Fill well greased muffin tins or paper muffin cups ½ full.
7. Bake 400 degrees until light golden brown—approximately 15-20 minutes.

Note: Can be made ahead of time. Freezes well.

BLUEBERRY
MUFFINS

Menu IV

California Sausage Bake

Top of the Morning Fruit Salad

with Whipped Topping

Toasted English Muffins

Coffee

California Sausage Bake

(for full flavor make day before and refrigerate overnight. Remove from refrigerator in advance and let come to room temperature before baking.)

Preparation time: 30 minutes   Cooking time: 45-60 minutes
Serves 8

8 slices day old white bread, cubed

2 lbs. sausage (hot or medium hot), cooked and drained

1½ cups grated sharp Cheddar cheese

6 eggs slightly beaten

2½ cups milk

1 T. brown sugar

¼ t. paprika

1 T. dried minced onion

¼ t. dry mustard

¼ t. salt

⅛ t. pepper

1 t. Worcestershire Sauce

⅛ t. Tabasco

1 4 oz. can mushrooms, drained

1. Preheat oven to 350 degrees.
2. Brown sausage and drain well.
3. Place half cubed bread in bottom of 9×13 inch baking dish. Spread half cooked sausage over bread. Top with half cheese. Repeat layers.
4. Mix together eggs, milk, brown sugar, paprika, onion, mustard, salt, pepper, Worcestershire, Tabasco, and mushrooms.
5. Pour over layered mixture.
6. Bake 350 degrees 45-60 minutes or until firm.

Top of the Morning Fruit Salad

(see rule for congealed salads, p. 238)

Preparation time: 10 minutes   Serves 12-14

2 15¼ oz. cans crushed pineapple

2 envelopes plain gelatin

½ cup water

2 cups pineapple juice from crushed pineapple

1 cup mayonnaise (no substitutes)

1 8 oz. package cream cheese, softened

1 4½ oz. package egg custard mix

4 individual packages instant Daiquiri mix

1 cup chopped pecans (optional)

1. Drain crushed pineapple and reserve juice, squeezing pineapple with hands to yield 2 cups juice.
2. Heat pineapple juice.
3. Soften gelatin in ½ cup water.
4. Add to hot pineapple juice and stir until dissolved.
5. Put mayonnaise, cream cheese, egg custard mix, Daiquiri mix, and pineapple-gelatin mixture into blender.
6. Blend on high until well mixed—about 40 seconds.
7. Pour blended mixture into mixing bowl, folding in crushed pineapple and nuts, if used.
8. Spoon into lightly oiled individual molds, a 9×12 Pyrex dish, or 1½ to 2 qt. salad mold or ring.

Whipped Topping

1 container whipped topping with Real Cream

1. Place in serving bowl beside salad.

TOASTED ENGLISH MUFFIN

Toasted English Muffins

Preparation time: 5 minutes   Cooking time: 6-8 minutes
Serves 8

8 English muffins   **1 jar marmalade**
Butter

1. Split English muffins, tearing in half to give coarse texture.
2. Butter each half generously.
3. Place 6 inches from broiler flame.
4. Broil 6-8 minutes or until light golden brown.
5. Serve with marmalade.

**Note: Wrap in foil and place in warm oven until ready
to serve if prepared in advance.**

Menu V

Icy Cold Cucumber Soup

Springtime-Summery Fruit Melange

with

Lime Sherbet

Piquant Fruit Salad Dressing

Party Ham Sandwiches

Iced Tea

Icy Cold Cucumber Soup

(serve in chilled cups or wine glasses as a first course
before brunch)

see P. ___31___ for recipe

(double for eight)

Springtime-Summery Fruit Melange
(served on individual dinner-sized plates)

Preparation time: 30 minutes   Serves 8-10

Choose 6-8 from the following season ripened, canned, or frozen fruits, preferably fresh fruits in season.

10 apricot halves

10 slices fresh or canned pineapple

1 large canteloupe or honeydew melon cut into rings or slices

1 quart strawberries

2 pounds grapes

8 pear halves

2 papayas cut into slices

6 fresh peaches cut into slices or 8-10 canned peach halves

4 Kiwi cut into slices

5 bananas split in halves*

2 mangos cut into slices

1 head leafy green lettuce

1. Choose fruits, wash, drain, and cut into appropriate sizes.
2. Place fruits in separate bowls, cover with Fruit Fresh syrup (see following recipe), and make airtight with plastic wrap. Refrigerate until ready to serve.
3. Wash and drain lettuce well. Wrap in paper towels, cover tightly with plastic wrap, and refrigerate.
4. At serving time drain liquid from fruit. Cover each plate with crisp lettuce and place fruit attractively around plate leaving room in center for compote of lime sherbet.
5. Place compote or glass dish of sherbet in center of each plate (see diagram, p. <u>208</u>)
6. Pass ham sandwiches and fruit salad dressing at table.

* Do not prepare until morning of brunch.

Fruit Fresh Syrup

(for preserving fresh fruits)

Makes enough for 1 quart of fresh fruit

2 t. Fruit Fresh   **3 T. water**

1. Dissolve Fruit Fresh in water and toss with 1 quart fruit.
2. Wrap tightly in plastic wrap or put in airtight containers until ready to use.

Lime Sherbet

(Prepare the day before and freeze)

Preparation time: 12 minutes   Serves 8

1 3½ oz. bottle green   **1 quart lime sherbet**
Maraschino cherries

1. Spoon lime sherbet into individual glass compotes or double paper baking cups.
2. Cover with plastic wrap or foil and freeze.
3. At serving time place in center of fruit filled plate, and garnish sherbet with green Maraschino cherries.

Piquant Fruit Salad

(make several days or a week before)

Preparation time: 10 minutes   Makes 2²/₃ cups

⅔ cup cider vinegar   **¼ t. Tabasco**
3 T. sugar   **2 cups corn or safflower**
1 t. dry mustard   **oil**
1 t. dried minced chives

1. Put vinegar, sugar, mustard, chives, and Tabasco in blender, or mix well by hand with a whisk.
2. Add 2 cups oil slowly, blending until thick.
3. Pour into attractive bottle or cruet to use for pouring at table.

Party Ham Sandwiches with Mustard Mayonnaise

(can be made the day before)

Preparation time: 15 minutes   Serves 8

1½ pounds thinly sliced ham bought from deli or grocery

2 loaves party rye bread

1. Spread each slice of bread liberally with mustard mayonnaise.
2. Add slivers of ham and top with another bread slice.
3. Cover with slightly moist dish towel, wrap securely in plastic wrap and refrigerate until serving time.
4. Pass on separate tray at table.

Mustard Mayonnaise

(keeps well for a month)

Preparation time: 7 minutes   Makes 2 cups

3 T. dry mustard
2 T. cider vinegar
⅛ t. Tabasco

½ t. horseradish
2 cups mayonnaise (no substitutes)

1. Dissolve mustard in vinegar.
2. Add Tabasco and horseradish.
3. Blend in mayonnaise and mix well.
4. Cover and refrigerate until ready to use.

DELECTABLE DESSERTS

Glamorous But Easy

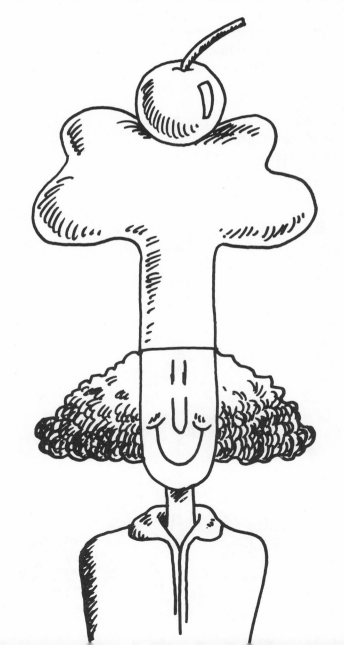

DELECTABLE DESSERTS

Chocolate Almond Pie

rich, rich … but oh, so good!

Preparation time: 15 minutes   Serves 6

1 6 oz. Ready Crust, graham cracker

4 Hershey bars with almonds (1.45 oz. each)

3 cups miniature marsh- mallows

¼ cup milk

1⅔ cups whipped topping with Real cream

1 2 oz. package slivered almonds, toasted*

2 t. Crème de Cacao (optional)

1. Place chocolate bars, marshmallows, and milk in sauce- pan and cook until thoroughly melted, stirring constantly with a whisk.
2. Pour mixture into cold bowl and place in freezer until cool — about 10 minutes.
3. Remove from freezer and fold in almonds, whipped topping, and Crème de Cacao.
4. Spoon into graham cracker crust, cover, and refrigerate several hours before serving.
5. At serving time, top with additional dollops of whipped topping and shaved chocolate.

* See P. __92__ for toasting almonds.

Fantastically Easy Mocha Pie

Preparation time: 10 minutes   Serves 6

1 6 oz. Ready Crust, chocolate flavored

1 quart coffee ice cream

4 Heath English Toffee bars (1¹⁄₁₆ oz. each)

2 cups whipped topping with Real cream

1 T. Kahlua liqueur (optional)

1. Place Heath bars in sturdy plastic sack and tie tightly.
2. Break into small pieces with hammer or handle edge of heavy kitchen utensil.
3. Spoon 1 quart coffee ice cream into pie crust.
4. Top with 2 cups whipped topping mixed with 1 T. Kahlua.
5. Sprinkle crumbled Heath bars over top of whipped cream.
6. Cover and freeze until ready to serve.

Grasshopper Pie

Preparation time: 11 minutes   Serves 6

1 6 oz. Ready Crust, chocolate flavored

4 cups miniature marsh-mallows

¼ cup plus 1 T. milk (or cream)

2 T. white Crème de Cacao

2 T. green Crème de Menthe

2 cups whipped topping with Real cream

1 cup whipped topping with Real cream for garnish

Chocolate curls (optional)

continued on next page

1. Combine marshmallows and milk in saucepan and cook until marshmallows are melted, stirring constantly.
2. Cool slightly.
3. Stir in liqueurs and 2 cups whipped cream topping. Whisk until well combined.
4. Spoon into prepared crust.
5. Refrigerate until firm—at least 3 hours.
6. When ready to serve, garnish with 1 cup whipped cream topping and shaved chocolate curls.

10-Minute Luscious Lemon Pie

Preparation time: 10 minutes   Serves 6

**1 can sweetened
  condensed milk**
**½ cup lemon juice
  (approximately 3 whole
  lemons)**
grated rind of 1 lemon

**1 6 oz. Ready Crust,
  graham cracker flavored**
**2 cups whipped topping
  with Real cream**

1. Grate lemon rind into mixing bowl.
2. Squeeze lemons and combine juice with rind and sweetened condensed milk.
3. Beat with whisk until all ingredients are well blended.
4. Spoon into graham cracker crust and refrigerate until filling is firm.
5. When firm, top with 2 cups whipped topping.

**Note: For that extra touch, garnish with thin slices of
  lemon and fresh fruit.**

Mile-High Frozen Strawberry Pie

Preparation time: 15 minutes   Serves 8

3 cups lightly toasted cocoanut*

½ cup butter or margarine

1 3 oz. package cream cheese, softened

½ cup sour cream

1 14 oz. can Eagle Brand sweetened condensed milk

3 T. bottled lemon juice

1 16 oz. package frozen sliced strawberries, thawed (or 2½ cups fresh, sliced) and undrained

2 cups whipped topping with Real cream

Additional fresh strawberries for garnish (optional)

1. Melt butter in saucepan.
2. Stir in toasted cocoanut and mix well.
3. Press cocoanut mixture into bottom and sides of pie pan. Place in freezer to chill.
4. In large bowl, beat cream cheese until fluffy.
5. Beat in Eagle Brand, sour cream, strawberries plus syrup, and lemon juice.
6. Fold in whipped topping.
7. Spoon into cocoanut crust, cover and freeze 4 hours or until firm.
8. Garnish with additional fresh strawberries.

* To toast cocoanut, preheat oven to 350 degrees. Spread cocoanut on a cookie sheet or anything fairly flat. Place in oven, stir occasionally, and toast about 8 minutes — until lightly browned.

Frozen Pina Colada Torte

(refreshing flavor and a natural cereal crust)

Preparation time: 12 minutes   Serves 8

**2 cups finely crushed
  100% natural cereal**
¼ cup light brown sugar
¼ cup melted butter
**3 cups Piña Colada
  sherbet**

**1 15½ oz. can crushed
  pineapple, drained**
**½ cup shredded, toasted
  cocoanut***

1. Put butter and sugar in saucepan and heat until melted.
2. Combine melted butter and sugar with 1½ cups cereal and mix well.
3. Spread cereal mixture in bottom of a 13 × 9 pyrex dish.
4. Spread 3 cups Piña Colada sherbet on top, mashing sherbet into cereal mixture with palm of hand.
5. Spread well drained pineapple on top of sherbet, topping with ½ cup cocoanut and remaining ½ cup cereal.
6. Freeze until ready to serve.

* See p. __218__ for toasting cocoanut.

Chocolate Mint Frozen Dessert

Preparation time: 10 minutes   Serves 6

1 6 oz. Ready Crust, chocolate flavored

1 quart Chocolate Mint ice cream

1 6 oz. package semi- sweet chocolate chips

2 T. milk (or cream)

1½ t. Mint Chocolate liqueur (optional)

1. Spoon Chocolate Mint ice cream into prepared pie shell.
2. Place in freezer.
3. Melt chocolate chips and milk in saucepan, stirring constantly.
4. Add liqueur, mix well, and remove from heat.
5. Cool slightly, placing in freezer for a couple of minutes if too hot.
6. Spread chocolate topping over frozen ice cream.
7. Cover and freeze until ready to serve.

Ice Creams with Imaginative Toppings

(What guest can resist a yummy concoction like these?)

Pineapple Sherbet	. . . . . . with	Cognac
Butter Pecan	. . . . . . with	Crème de Banana
Chocolate	. . . . . . with	Crème de Almond or Amaretto
Chocolate	. . . . . . with	Crème de Cacao
Cherry Vanilla	. . . . . . with	Wild Cherry Brandy
Coffee	. . . . . . with	Curacao
Coffee	. . . . . . with	Kahlúa
Vanilla	. . . . . . with	Dark or Light Rum
Vanilla	. . . . . . with	B and B
Vanilla	. . . . . . with	Crème de Menthe (green)
Vanilla	. . . . . . with	Tia Maria

Or take a scoop of ice cream or sherbet and create your own!

Sicilian Chocolate Torte

(intriguingly different)

(better flavor if made 24 hours in advance; keeps well
in refrigerator for a week or can be made ahead and
frozen)

Preparation time: 15–18 minutes   Serves 18–20

**1 16 oz. Sara Lee All
Butter Pound Cake
1 15 oz. carton Ricotta
cheese**

**¼ cup powdered sugar
4 T. orange flavored
liqueur (Triple Sec or
other orange flavored
liqueur)**

1. Slice cake horizontally into 4 even slabs.
2. Combine Ricotta cheese, powdered sugar, and liqueur
   and beat by hand until well mixed (1–2 minutes).
3. Place bottom slice of cake on flat surface and spread with
   ¹/₃ of Ricotta mixture. Repeat layers until all cake slices
   are used up. End with a cake slice on top.
4. Press loaf firmly together and be sure all sides are even.
5. If weather is warm, refrigerate until filling is set before
   icing.

continued on next page

Frosting for Sicilian Torte

1 16.5 oz. can Creamy Deluxe Ready to Spread Chocolate Frosting
1 T. hot water

1 T. instant coffee
1 t. vanilla
1 2 oz. package toasted slivered almonds (optional)*

1. Dissolve 1 T. coffee in 1 T. hot water.
2. In a small mixing bowl, combine coffee, vanilla, and frosting.
3. Beat until mixture is smooth and ingredients well combined—about 1 minute.
4. Frost tops and sides of torte, swirling chocolate decoratively.
5. Sprinkle with toasted almonds. Press any loose almonds gently into frosting.
6. Cover and refrigerate.

* See p. <u>92</u> for toasting almonds.

Golden Rum Cake

(stays fresh and moist for over a week!)

Preparation time: 10 minutes   Baking time: 1 hour
Serves 10–12

1 18½ oz. box yellow cake mix with pudding
3 eggs
½ cup cold water

⅓ cup corn oil
½ cup dark rum
1 cup chopped pecans

1. Preheat oven to 325 degrees.
2. Grease and flour a 10″ tube or bundt pan.
3. Mix together: cake mix, eggs, water, oil, rum, and pecans.
4. Blend well either by hand or with electric mixer.
5. Pour into greased pan and bake 325 degrees for 1 hour.

continued on next page

Topping

(can be spooned over either hot or cold cake)

¼ lb. butter (1 stick)   **1 cup sugar**
¼ cup water   **¼ cup dark rum**

1. Mix topping ingredients together and heat until butter is melted and sugar is absorbed, stirring constantly.
2. Prick cake with fork on all sides and top.
3. Spoon topping over cake waiting a few moments in between spoonings for topping to be absorbed.

Orange Nectar Cake

Preparation time: 6 minutes   Cooking time: 1 hour
Serves 18-20

1 18.5 oz. box Deluxe Orange Supreme cake mix

1 3¾ oz. box vanilla pudding and pie filling mix

4 eggs
½ cup corn oil
¼ cup Apricot Brandy
¾ cup apricot nectar (1 5½ oz. can)

1. Preheat oven to 325 degrees.
2. Grease and flour a 10″ bundt pan (or any pan of equivalent size).
3. In mixing bowl combine cake mix, pudding mix, eggs, oil, Apricot Brandy, and apricot nectar.
4. Mix until all ingredients are well blended.
5. Pour into bundt pan and cook 1 hour at 325 degrees or until cake tests done.
6. Invert on a cake plate and prick all over before spooning on glaze.

continued on next page

Glaze

4 T. butter   **⅓ cup Apricot Brandy**
¾ cup sugar   **¼ cup water**

1. Heat butter, sugar, and water in small saucepan until butter is melted and sugar is dissolved.
2. Remove from heat, add Apricot Brandy, mixing well.
3. Prick cake on top and sides with fork.
4. Spoon glaze slowly over cake, letting cake absorb liquid before adding additional glaze.

Note: Cake keeps well for a week to 10 days. Freezes well.

Pineapple Upside-Down Cake

Preparation time: 10 minutes   Cooking time: 30 minutes
Makes 1 8″ round cake

¼ cup butter (½ stick)   **1 9 oz. box yellow cake mix**
1 cup light brown sugar
1 15 oz. can pineapple   **1 egg**
slices, well drained   **1 cup water**
1 cup pecans (optional)

1. Preheat oven to 350 degrees.
2. Place ¼ cup butter in 8″ round pan and put in oven to melt.
3. Combine cake mix, egg, and water, stirring until well mixed.
4. Remove cake pan from oven and tilt in all directions to coat butter evenly.
5. Sprinkle 1 cup light brown sugar over melted butter.
6. Lay pineapple slices over brown sugar and sprinkle evenly with pecans.
7. Pour cake batter over pineapple.
8. Cook 350 degrees for 30 minutes or until cake tests done.
9. Cool 10 minutes.
10. Invert on cake plate and garnish with red cherries for color.

Apple Crunch

Preparation time: 15 minutes   Serves 12

Filling

2 20 oz. cans sliced apples in water
¼ cup flour
1 cup white sugar

¼ t. salt
½ t. cinnamon
⅛ t. nutmeg

1. In large saucepan, combine and bring to a boil: undrained apples, flour, sugar, salt, cinnamon, and nutmeg.
2. Reduce heat to a simmering boil, stirring constantly.
3. Cook 5–6 minutes or until mixture has thickened slightly.
4. Pour into an 8 × 12 baking dish.

Crumb Topping

¼ cup plus 2 T. melted butter
1 cup flour
½ cup plus 2 T. packed light brown sugar
½ cup quick oats

½ t. cinnamon
½ cup crushed cornflakes (about 1½ cups whole cornflakes)
½ t. baking soda

1. preheat oven to 425 degrees.
2. In mixing bowl combine flour, brown sugar, oats, cinnamon, crushed cornflakes, and baking soda. Mix well.
3. Pour melted butter into crumb mixture and stir until mixture resembles coarse crumbs.
4. Sprinkle crumb mixture evenly over top of apples.
5. Bake 425 degrees for 15–18 minutes — until thoroughly heated. Can run under the broiler for 2–3 minutes if not brown enough.

Note: Serve warm with vanilla ice cream.

Raspberry-Walnut Fluff

Preparation time: 10 minutes   Serves 8–10

1 6 oz. package raspberry Jello

2 cups hot water

2 10 oz. packages frozen raspberries

½ cup sherry

2 cups whipped topping with Real Cream

1 cup walnuts, chopped

1. Dissolve Jello in hot water.
2. Add frozen raspberries and stir until raspberries break apart
3. Remove from heat. Add sherry and nuts.
4. Fold in whipped topping.
5. Fill small bowls, wine glasses, or one large glass bowl with raspberry mixture.
6. Refrigerate several hours until set.
7. Garnish with additional dollop of whipped topping when served.

Strawberries with Crème Of Liqueur Almond

Preparation time: 10 minutes   Serves 4–6

2 cups (1 pint) fresh strawberries, washed and stemmed*

1 15 oz. can blueberries, drained

1. Divide fruit evenly among 4 compotes or glass bowls.
2. Cover with plastic wrap and refrigerate until ready to use.
3. At serving time spoon Almond Cream over fruit.

*May substitute bananas, fresh or canned pineapple chunks for strawberries.

continued on next page

Almond Cream

(keeps well for a month in refrigerator)

1 cup sour cream   **2 T. almond liqueur**
3 T. powdered sugar

1. Combine sour cream, powdered sugar, and almond liqueur.
2. Stir to blend well.
3. Cover and refrigerate until ready to use.
4. At serving time, spoon cream over fruit and garnish with a fresh mint sprig.

The Flambé Show

Bananas Foster.....Cherries Jubilee

Dazzle your guests with a flambé show! Flaming desserts have an intimidating reputation, but actually are very simple. Follow the basic rules and you're sure to impress your guests.

1. Make sure ice cream is hard before hot sauce is poured over. Freeze individual portions on a plate, cookie sheet, etc. several hours before serving.
2. Heat liqueur separately before adding it to the dessert.
3. Do not allow liqueur to boil.
4. Make sure bananas or cherries plus liquid are hot before adding warm liqueur.
5. Pour warmed liqueur evenly over dessert and ignite immediately.
6. No chafing dish? Light dessert in kitchen using a skillet and make a grand entrance to the table.

REMEMBER...Both liqueur and dessert ingredients *MUST BE WARM* before flame will ignite.

Cherries Jubilee

Preparation time: 10 minutes   Serves 6

1 15½ oz. can pitted Bing Cherries

¼ cup Brandy

2 T. Kirsch

6 scoops Vanilla ice cream

1. Heat can of cherries in chafing dish or skillet.
2. Pour warm Brandy over and ignite.
3. When flame has died out, stir in 2 T. Kirsch.
4. Spoon warm sauce over individual scoops of ice cream.

Note: If you do not wish to flame the cherries, soak cherries in Brandy 3-4 hours in advance. Add Kirsch at last and heat until just warm.

Bananas Foster

Preparation time: 10 minutes   Serves 2

1 large ripe banana

1 t. bottled lemon juice

3 T. light brown sugar

2 T. butter

¼ t. cinnamon

2 T. Banana liqueur

2 T. Rum

2 scoops vanilla ice cream

1. Peel bananas and halve lengthwise.
2. Sprinkle with lemon juice.
3. Melt sugar and butter in chafing dish or skillet. Stir in cinnamon.
4. Add bananas and cook until barely tender, spooning juice over constantly. About 5 minutes.
5. Add warm Banana liqueur and warm Rum and set aflame, basting bananas until flame dies out.
6. Transfer bananas to flat dessert plates or salad plates with a scoop of vanilla ice cream on the side. Spoon sauce over bananas and ice cream.

STASHING AWAY THE BASICS

Party Countdown

Don't feel overwhelmed whatever the occasion! Today's casual lifestyle makes having friends a delight, careful planning the key.

Do

1. Be orderly — make lists, write down schedules.
2. Decide on a menu.
3. Read recipes carefully and make a grocery list of ingredients specified.
4. Grocery shop well in advance, refrigerating perishables, and preparing ahead recipes which freeze well.

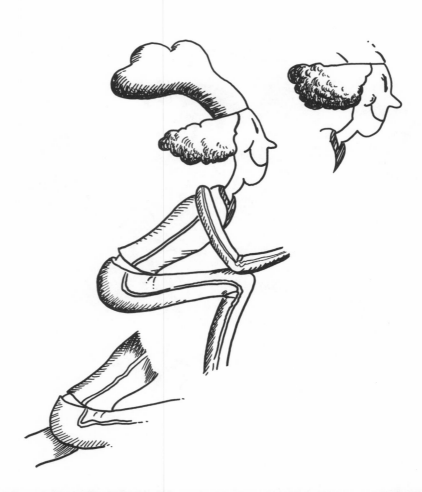

Decorative Tables Ingenuity Running Riot

Nobody has to display a grandiose collection of china, crystal, and silver to set an eye-appealing table. Any object that is attractive elsewhere can be used...wondrous table arrangements whipped up out of simple odds and ends.

Flowers and greenery in crystal, flowers and greenery in baskets...

Spectacular fruit and/or vegetable centerpieces good enough to eat!

1) broccoli or green onions standing upright and tied with a piece of brightly colored yarn.
2) cucumber
3) cherry tomatoes
4) radishes
5) bermuda onion or fresh turnip
6) acorn squash
7) avocado

... Try ...

Candle creations from floating wicks in water to dazzling galaxies of towering tapers!

An arrangement of candles in varying heights with mirrored glass as a base. Ring with pine or ivy.

A single dramatic bloom—magnolia, water lily, dahlia, amaryllis, camellia—floating in a water-filled glass bowl…

Accent the seasons…Fill a giant coffee mug, bean pot, or pitcher with…
Spring and summer—fresh and wild flowers, budding foliage.
Winter—bare branches, evergreens, red holly berries, and mistletoe.
Fall—Harvest golds and flaming reds of autumn leaves.

Tiny pots of geraniums, begonias, or ivy with a candle in the center of each...

A pyramid of handsome oranges sprigged with greenery...

A fat yellow candle in a hurricane lamp flanked by a double ring of lemons (braced with toothpicks) and green leaves...

Tumbling out of a straw basket—shiny red apples and richly hued purple grapes laced with ivy sprigs…

A collection of sea shells, interspersed with bunches of pansies, petunias, or violets…

A piece of sculpture surrounded with ivy and low burning candles…

Note: Except on buffet table, arrangements should be low so that guests can see over them.
Keep floral clay and oasis on hand for flower arrangements, soaking oasis in deep water thoroughly before use.

Setting The Scene

The Basics

(1) Salad Plate (2) Salad Fork (3) Dinner Fork
(4) Dinner Plate (5) Dinner Knife (6) Teaspoon*
(7) Water Glass (8) Wine Glass*

* May be omitted

Basics Elaborated

(1) Salad Fork (2) Dinner Fork (3) Dinner Plate
(4) Dinner Knife (5) Teaspoon (6) Soup Spoon*
(7) Wine Glass (8) Water Glass (9) Bread and Butter plate
(10) Bread and Butter knife (11) Salad Plate

* If serving soup as first course

COOKWARE YOU CAN'T DO WITHOUT

1 medium saucepan
   (2 quarts)
1 large saucepan (3 quarts)
1 large kettle or pan
   (10 quarts)
1 10-inch skillet with lid

Coffee pot
Electric blender
Electric frying pan
Assorted casserole or
   baking dishes

EQUIPMENT

Cooking fork
Cooking spoon
Spatula
Wire Whisk
Garlic press
Cheese grater
Rubber spatula

Mixing bowl set
Colander
Measuring spoons
Graduated measuring cups
Glass measuring cup
Good set of knives
Vegetable peeler

NICE TO HAVE. . .

Nice to have. . .
Cookie sheets
Muffin tin
Ramekins or individual pyrex casseroles
Chafing dish

THE ESSENTIAL GADGETS

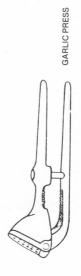

GARLIC PRESS

WIRE WHISKS

Cutting tools from left to right: chef's knife, ham slicer, paring knife.

Glass Measuring Cup: For measuring liquids. Read the measurement at eye level.

⅛ t   ¼ t   ½ t   1 t   1 T

⅛ cup   ¼ cup   ⅓ cup   ½ cup   1 cup

Important Rules

FOR CONGEALING SALADS

1. Use 1 T. or 1 envelope plain gelatin to 2 cups liquid.
2. Soak 1 T. gelatin in ¼ cup cold water for about 2-3 minutes to soften or until gelatin has absorbed all the liquid.
3. Add gelatin to 1¾ cups boiling water or juice and stir until dissolved.

TO DOUBLE GELATIN RECIPES

1. Instead of using 4 cups of liquid, reduce to 3¾ cups total liquid if single recipe calls for 2 cups.

MOLDING AND UNMOLDING CONGEALED SALADS

1. Lightly oil mold with mayonnaise or cooking oil before adding salad.
2. To unmold: moisten outside of mold with warm water until salad is loose from sides and bottom. Hold plate beneath mold and invert onto plate.
3. NO SALAD MOLDS? Use paper cups or short fat juice glasses for individual molds. Use mixing bowls or a cooking pan for larger molds.

HOW TO HARD-COOK AN EGG

1. Place eggs in sauce pan.
2. Cover with cold water.
3. Place pan on medium high heat and cover.
4. Bring water to a boil.
5. Reduce heat and let water simmer for 17-18 minutes.
6. Immediately run cold water over cooked eggs to stop cooking process.

Measurements, Weights, Equivalents

MEASUREMENTS THAT HELP

3 teaspoons	=	1 tablespoon
2 tablespoons	=	1 ounce
4 tablespoons	=	¼ cup
8 tablespoons	=	½ cup
4 ounces	=	½ cup
16 tablespoons	=	1 cup
8 ounces	=	1 cup
1 cup	=	½ pint
2 cups	=	1 pint
16 ounces	=	1 pound
2 pints	=	1 quart
4 cups	=	1 quart
4 quarts	=	1 gallon

METRIC CONVERSION TABLE

WEIGHT

To Change	*To*	*Multiply by*
Ounces	Grams	30.0
Pounds	Kilograms	.48

VOLUME

To Change	*To*	*Multiply by*
Teaspoons	Milliliters	5.0
Tablespoons	Milliliters	15.0
Cups	Milliliters	250.0
Cups	Liters	.25
Pints	Liters	.5
Quarts	Liters	1.0
Gallons	Liters	4.0

LENGTH

To Change	*To*	*Multiply by*
Inches	Millimeters	25.0
Inches	Centimeters	2.5
Feet	Centimeters	30.0
Yards	Meters	0.9

LIQUID MEASUREMENTS*
(nearest convenient equivalents)

1 T.	=	15 ml.
¼ cup	=	62.5 ml.
⅓ cup	=	83.3 ml.
½ cup	=	125 ml.
1 cup	=	250 ml. (¼ liter)
2 cups	=	500 ml. (½ liter)
1 quart	=	1,000 ml. (1 liter)
1 gallon	=	4,000 ml. (4 liters)

WEIGHTS
(nearest convenient equivalents)

½ ounce	=	15 grams
1 ounce	=	30 grams
4 ounces (¼ lb.)	=	114 grams
8 ounces (½ lb.)	=	227 grams
16 ounces (1 lb.)	=	464 grams

Note to remember:
100 grams is slightly less than ¼ lb.
250 grams is slightly more than ½ lb.
500 grams is slightly more than 1 lb.
1,000 grams is slightly more than 2 lbs. or 1 kilogram

*Taken from "Units of Weights and Measures", U.S. Government Printing Office, Washington, D.C.

AVERAGE CAN SIZES

Can Size	Weight	Cupfuls
8 oz.	8 oz.	1
No. 1	11 oz.	1⅓
No. 1½	16 oz.	2
No. 2	20 oz.	2½
No. 2½	28 oz.	3½
No. 3	33 oz.	4
No. 10	106 oz.	13

HELPFUL EQUIVALENTS

1 stick butter	½ cup
2 cups butter	1 pound
1 square chocolate	1 ounce
1 lemon	2-3 T. juice
2 cups diced meat	1 pound meat
½ cup rice	2 cups cooked rice
9 saltines crushed	1 cup crumbs
3 medium apples	1 pound or 2⅓ cups
1 cup grated cheese	¼ pound or 4 ounces

INDEX